Hiking Waterfalls
Yosemite National Park

Hiking Waterfalls
Yosemite
National Park

A Guide to the Park's Greatest Waterfalls

Suzanne Swedo

FALCONGUIDES

GUILFORD, CONNECTICUT

To Steven Bakos and Marta Kis
for their fabulous photography, technical expertise,
love of Yosemite, and treasured friendship

FALCONGUIDES®

An imprint of The Rowman & Littlefield Publishing Group, Inc.
4501 Forbes Blvd., Ste. 200
Lanham, MD 20706
www.rowman.com
Falcon and FalconGuides are registered trademarks and Make Adventure Your Story is a trademark of The Rowman & Littlefield Publishing Group, Inc.

Distributed by NATIONAL BOOK NETWORK

Photos by Suzanne Swedo unless otherwise noted

Maps by The Roman & Littlefield Publishing Group, Inc.

British Library Cataloguing in Publication Information available

Library of Congress Cataloging-in-Publication Data available

ISBN 978-1-4930-3448-2 (paperback)
ISBN 978-1-4930-3449-9 (e-book)

∞™ The paper used in this publication meets the minimum requirements of American National Standard for Information Sciences—Permanence of Paper for Printed Library Materials, ANSI/NISO Z39.48-1992.

Printed in the United States of America

Contents

Acknowledgments viii
Introduction ix
How to Use This Guide xiii
Life in Yosemite xvi
Geology.. xviii
History xx
Leave No Trace... xxii
For Your Safety xxiv
Trail Finder xxix
Map Legend xxxiv

Yosemite Valley Waterfalls 1
    1. Vernal Fall Bridge.. 5
    2. Top of Nevada Fall via John Muir Trail 7
    3. Vernal and Nevada Falls from the Mist Trail 11
    4. Silver Apron 15
    5. Lower Yosemite Falls.. 18
    6. Upper Yosemite Falls from Yosemite Valley 21
    7. Yosemite Falls from Tioga Road 24
    8. Bridalveil Fall 28
    9. Silver Strand Fall.. 32
  10. Ribbon Fall 35
  11. Cascade Creek Falls 38
  12. Upper Cascade Creek Cascades 42
  13. Sentinel Fall.. 47
  14. Illilouette Fall 51
  15. Staircase Fall 54
  16. Lehamite Fall 56
  17. Upper Snow Creek Falls 58
  18. Horsetail Fall 63
  19. Royal Arch Cascade 66
  20. Basket Dome Fall... 69

Waterfalls of the Western Foothills.................................... 73
  21. Red Rock Falls 75
  22. Corlieu Falls 79
  23. Foresta Falls 82
  24. Little Nellie Falls 87
  25. Preston Falls... 90

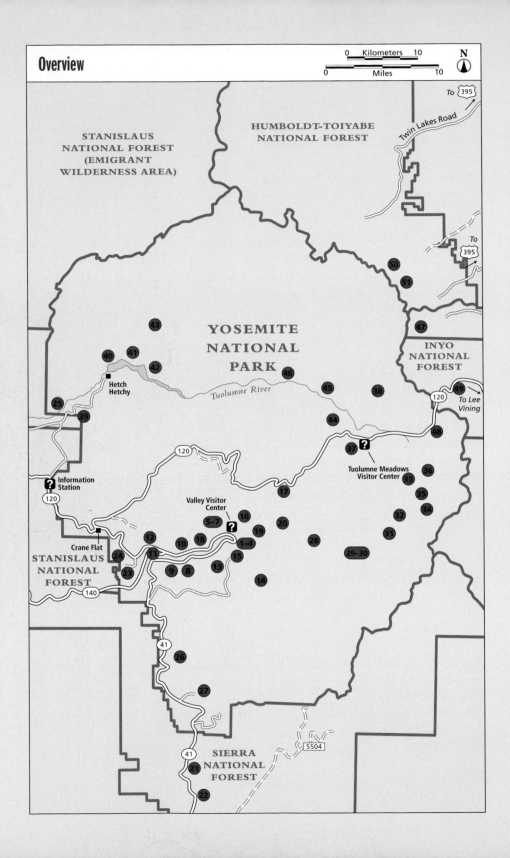

Overview

STANISLAUS
NATIONAL FOREST
(EMIGRANT
WILDERNESS AREA)

HUMBOLDT-TOIYABE
NATIONAL FOREST

To 395

Twin Lakes Road

To
395

YOSEMITE
NATIONAL
PARK

Tuolumne River

INYO
NATIONAL
FOREST

To Lee
Vining

Hetch
Hetchy

Tuolumne Meadows
Visitor Center

Information
Station

Valley Visitor
Center

Crane Flat

STANISLAUS
NATIONAL
FOREST

5504

SIERRA
NATIONAL
FOREST

Wawona-Area Falls **93**
  26. Alder Creek Falls 95
  27. Chilnualna Falls 99

Waterfalls in the Heart of the Park **103**
  28. Merced River Falls 105
  29. Bunnell Cascade 110
  30. Merced Lake Cascades 115
  31. Fletcher Creek Cascades 122
  32. Vogelsang Cascades 128

Waterfalls of the Tuolumne Meadows Region **133**
  33. Rafferty Creek Falls 135
  34. Kuna Falls 140
  35. Ireland Lake Falls 143
  36. Lyell Fork Cascades 146
  37. Dana Fork Cascades 150
  38. Young Lakes Falls 152

Hetch Hetchy Waterfalls **157**
  39. Carlon Falls 159
  40. Tueeulala Falls 162
  41. Wapama Falls 166
  42. Rancheria Falls 170
  43. Lake Vernon Cascade 173

Grand Canyon of the Tuolumne River Waterfalls **177**
  44. Tuolumne Falls and the White Cascade 179
  45. Waterwheel Falls via LeConte and California Falls 184
  46. The Grand Canyon of the Tuolumne 189

Waterfalls of the Sierra Crest **195**
  47. Mill Creek Falls 197
  48. Parker Pass Falls 202
  49. Ellery Lake Falls 207
  50. West Lake Falls 211
  51. Cooney Lake Falls 217

Bibliography 221
About the Author 222

Acknowledgments

Thanks to the many park rangers and other personnel and volunteers of the National Park Service in Yosemite who have been so generous with their time and assistance, especially Mark Fincher, who knows everything there is to know about the trails of Yosemite. Also to Kylie Chappell, Cassie May, Adonia Ripple, Pete Devine, and everyone at the Yosemite Conservancy, whose purpose it is to initiate and support interpretation, education, research, and scientific and environmental programs in Yosemite.

For their aid and encouragement and plain good company in the field, thanks also to Joellyn Acree, Andrea Canapary, Mari Carlos, Erica Crawford, Ed DeLeon-ardis, Minh Duong, Melinda Goodwater, Marissa Ortega-Welch, Fumiaki Nakamura, Sherry Rogers, Celia Ronis, and Sandy Steinman. And for the Yosemite toad, Nora Livingston.

Special thanks also to David Legere at FalconGuides for his endless patience.

Introduction

What is so fascinating about falling water? We travel all over the world at great effort and expense to watch water abruptly change elevation and give names to the places where a river or stream does that in some dramatic way. We take countless photographs of them, paint pictures of them, sometimes consider them sacred. Maybe it's just because water is such an essential component of our lives and our planet. We seem to be drawn to extreme topography and violent movement. The roar and power of great quantities of water thundering over a cliff into empty space is exhilarating and scary at the same time.

Waterfalls are associated with myths and legends in cultures around the world, including those in Yosemite. They are the places of spirits, sometimes beneficial but often malignant, luring people who come too close to their death.

Yet, we know that falling water transforms the air around it, refreshing the atmosphere, generating negative ions that not only counter air pollution but are said to influence our emotional states in positive ways, energizing us, banishing irritability and depression.

Some Definitions

There doesn't seem to be any agreement among hydrologists (or anybody else) about what it means to be a waterfall. How many vertical feet must water fall to be counted? How extreme must the slope be? What counts as the top of a waterfall, what counts as the bottom? Many streams transition from stream to waterfall gradually, rolling over a smooth rounded surface before becoming truly vertical. Sometimes water flows freely until it strikes a cone of rubble created by the action of the water or ice itself before the fall becomes a cascade, then becomes horizontal when it meets the valley floor or joins another stream.

How do we tell a waterfall from a cascade? The *Dictionary of Geological Terms* defines cascade as "a series of small closely spaced waterfalls or very steep rapids." It defines waterfall as "a point in the course of a stream or river where the water descends perpendicularly or nearly so." That helps . . . a little. It doesn't say how much elevation a stream running steeply downhill must lose in order to be called a cascade. Then there are slides, where a substantial stream of water may slip down a steep slope for hundreds of feet without losing contact with the land. For our purposes, these spectacular waterslides count as waterfalls too.

For our purposes as true waterfall lovers, size doesn't count. A few falls included here are less than 20 feet tall but have some quality that grabs your attention, makes

▶ Waterfalls can confuse our senses. Stand and stare at a waterfall for 20 to 30 seconds, then shift your gaze to a nearby stationary object. It will appear to be moving in the opposite direction.

you stop and smile or take a photo. The largest fall in Yosemite is 2,425 feet, but as a matter of fact, it is a combination of three waterfalls. It isn't always possible to say where a fall begins and ends or what to call the top and what to call the bottom, or it simply might never have been measured, so we'll say those are undetermined or indeterminate.

You might also notice that maps and text may distinguish fall (singular) from falls (plural). The difference is not arbitrary. A waterfall such as Ribbon Fall is a single more or less uninterrupted flow. On the other hand, Yosemite Falls is made up of three components: two waterfalls separated by a series of cascades in the middle.

Many of the falls you will find here are not named on the topo map; some have names used by local folks, and if they are widespread, we'll use them too. We will call those with no official title at all by the stream that feeds them or some special feature that describes them.

Why Yosemite Has the Best Waterfalls

Whatever it is that draws us to waterfalls, Yosemite is one of the best places on earth to see them. It has the greatest number, some of the biggest (two of them are among the tallest in the world), and surely the most scenic. And (for better or worse) they are close to large population centers and easily accessible. It's impossible to count with any accuracy the number of waterfalls, cascades, and slides here—there are surely thousands. Some of them flow all year, others flow only for a season, still others are ephemeral.

It is because of its geographical position, its geological history, and its climate that Yosemite has so many fabulous waterfalls. Granitic rocks make up 95 percent of Yosemite. One of their defining features is their massive structure. Indeed, El Capitan at the western end of the valley is said to be the largest unbroken monolithic hunk of rock in the world. This sort of rock forms huge solid cliffs with sharp right-angled edges and few joints or cracks, the kind of terrain that makes the best waterfalls.

Part of the Sierra Nevada range, thrust up by movement of tectonic plates, eventually rose enough to trap moist air from the Pacific, turning it to snow, then ice, as the Pleistocene epoch arrived. And the Sierra Nevada range, of which Yosemite is part, is located at the edge of a continent exposed to westerly winds that provided enough moisture to produce glaciers several thousand feet thick as the climate cooled several times during the recent geologic history of the Pleistocene.

While Yosemite's falls are most spectacular, they aren't all there all the time. The Sierra Nevada has a Mediterranean climate, characterized by cool, wet winters and hot, dry summers. There are fairly frequent summer afternoon thundershowers, but 95 percent of Yosemite's moisture comes from winter snowfall. Furthermore, its geologic history includes several advances and retreats of ice sheets that over the last 2 million years or so have scraped away vegetation and soil that help to retain water in

◀ STEVEN BAKOS

the high country. The result is that once the winter snow has melted there and flowed away over the cliffs in patterns that delight us, there is no more moisture available to keep water running until the next winter's snow. Unfortunately, that means that during late July and August when most people visit, the big waterfalls are shrinking and the smaller ones are dry. Waterfalls in Yosemite are best from April into July.

The Sierra Nevada still hosts a few small glaciers, remnants of the Little Ice Age of AD 1700 to 1900, but these are diminishing rapidly. In fact, there is only one active glacier left in Yosemite, the Lyell Glacier, which is itself shrinking fast.

HINTS FOR WATERFALL WATCHERS IN YOSEMITE: Get there early in the year for the falls at lower elevations like Yosemite Valley and Hetch Hetchy. If you are a backpacker, the high country may be inaccessible, with roads closed well into June, but falls will be flowing. As summer progresses, you might have to seek higher and higher country.

How to Use This Guide

The purpose of this guide is to help you enjoy Yosemite's finest and probably most famous features, its waterfalls; where to find them, what gives each its special character, and how much time and effort you will need to expend to reach each one. It offers a preview of what you are likely to see and experience along the way, including the geological features that produce and influence waterfalls, along with the trees, birds, flowers, and mammals that are guaranteed to enrich your journey.

All of the hikes in this book are on trails or on occasional abandoned roadways. None of them involve extensive cross-country travel or scrambling over challenging terrain beyond a few yards of bushwhacking to get a better view.

A few of these waterfalls require very little hiking but are included because you will certainly notice them and will want to know something about them. The rule: To truly experience a waterfall, even if only to check it off your list, you must expend at least a few steps, whenever possible, to hear the trickle or the roar, smell the moisture, feel the spray, or at least to seek out the best possible viewpoint you can find safely. A few of them are inaccessible on foot, but some are so special that hikes just to see them from a distance are included in this book.

Waterfall collectors: You don't get to count the waterfalls you glimpsed from a moving car.

Nobody can say how many waterfalls there are in Yosemite; it all depends on when you are there. Some flow all year, many are ephemeral, alive for only a few weeks, many flow from late winter through spring, while some appear at the beginning of late winter's snowmelt and continue throughout most of the summer.

Trail descriptions of more extended hikes are intended to be used along with the US Geological Survey topographic maps available at wilderness outfitting and sporting goods stores, at visitor centers and shops in Yosemite, and through the USGS at (888) ASK-USGS or www.usgsstore@usgs.gov. In many cases the free maps you will receive at park entrances or can pick up at a visitor center are all you need.

Each trail description opens with a short characterization of the fall, why it's worth your time and effort to visit it, whether it is free-falling or a cascade, whether it's ephemeral or flows year-round, and what the highlights and expectations are for the hike. The statistical section provides a quick reference to the characteristics of the waterfall and the hike. (This section may be omitted or abbreviated for a few of the very short hikes where they are not relevant.)

First comes the **Height** of the fall, when it is known. Many falls have never been measured, their heights only estimated. For many it's impossible to say where the waterfall actually starts and ends; it may begin with a slide over rounded rock before it enters freefall. Some waterfalls drop in sections, bouncing from one ledge to another, so that nobody can agree on just how many waterfalls there are. Many dissolve into mist before they reach the ground, some reach the ground at certain times of the year, and some simply disappear.

Then comes the **Start** of the hike, sometimes but not always marked with a trailhead sign.

The **Distance** of the hike is described in miles. You'll find out whether the route can be done as a loop, where you return to the place you started without retracing your steps; an out-and-back hike, in which you return to the trailhead the same way you came; or a shuttle hike, in which you begin at one trailhead and end at another, requiring two vehicles, a shuttle bus, or another driver to pick you up or deposit you at either end.

Elevation change will give you some idea of how much climbing and descending you can expect, both out and back or as a loop. But don't forget that there may be many ups and downs between the lowest and highest elevations.

The **Difficulty** rating is bound to be interpreted differently by hikers in varying degrees of physical condition, including their adaptability to high elevation. In general, easy trails can be negotiated by anybody who can walk. (A few are wheelchair accessible.) Moderate trails are of greater length or involve some elevation gain and loss, and may challenge those who are not accustomed to much physical activity. Strenuous hikes are for experienced hikers who are physically fit.

Seasons refers to the times of year that the fall is usually flowing, along with the time that the trails to them are open and safe to use and the roads to trailheads are usually open.

Nearest facilities refers to sources of supplies or contact with emergency services nearest the trailhead.

Permits are required for all overnight trips in the Yosemite Wilderness. Permit procedures and quotas are subject to change, so always check with the National Park Service (www.nps.gov/yose) for updates. A certain number can be reserved online in advance; the rest are first-come, first-served at wilderness centers in the park. Permits are not required for day hikes (except for climbing Half Dome).

Maps list the relevant names of USGS quads that will be useful for each hike. While our maps give you a general idea of the hike, it's a good idea to carry these more detailed maps with you for safety. For many of the shorter day hikes, the free maps provided by the park service are adequate.

Special considerations describe important safety or weather information.

Miles and Directions are landmarks on the trail, usually trail junctions. The distances are based on the official National Park Service measurements, but the park service cautions hikers to be aware that trails have been rerouted over the years to avoid obstacles like rockslides or washouts or to protect fragile vegetation in boggy meadows. The signs marking these trails have not always been corrected. Sometimes new signs will have been added to a trail but not to junctions along the way, so you will find that the miles don't always add up. Still, I have walked every trail in this book and have found none of the stated mileage between points to be inaccurate for more than a quarter mile.

Name changes: Since the park has changed concessionaires, there have been some very controversial changes of the names of commercial buildings in Yosemite. Many longtime Yosemite visitors still think of the original names as the "real" ones and continue to use them. People coming to Yosemite for the first time may not realize that some of the current names are recently acquired and often do not correspond to all maps and signposts. The name changes have met some resistance, and lawsuits are flying in all directions. The issue may be tied up in court for a long time so the changes might or might not be permanent. For the purposes of this book, we'll use both names, with one or the other in parentheses.

The *Yosemite Guide* newspaper you receive when you enter the park does list the current name changes. The ones you will see most often are:

Old name: The Ahwahnee Hotel; new name: The Majestic Yosemite Hotel

Old name: Curry Village; new name: Half Dome Village

Old name: The Wawona Hotel; new name: The Big Trees Lodge

Old name: Badger Pass; new name: Yosemite Ski and Snowboard Area

Life in Yosemite

Yosemite is a hiker's paradise because of its wonderful diversity. The range is only about 400 by 70 miles in extent and is mostly gray, granitic rock, yet every nook and cranny, and every stream drainage or mountain peak, is different from the rest. The main reason for this variety is Yosemite's wide range of elevation. Extremes of topography lead to extremes of weather, temperature, and soil. These in turn provide habitats for a wide variety of plants and animals. More than 1,300 species of flowering plants, 223 kinds of birds, and 77 kinds of mammals are found here. Summer days in the western foothills can reach 100°F; winter nights at the crest of the range may be 30°F below zero. The foothills may receive as little as 15 inches of precipitation in a year while the forests at 8,000 feet may get 65 feet. Still, the Sierra Nevada is a gentle wilderness to hike because 95 percent of its precipitation falls as winter snow. Summers are usually sunny and dry, and though thundershowers can be expected in July and August at higher elevations, they are usually of short duration.

The hiking season can begin as early as April in the western foothills between elevations of 2,000 and 4,000 feet. The rolling hills are covered with a mixture of shrubby chaparral and oak woodland, green and carpeted with flowers usually through May, becoming hotter and drier later in the season. As elevations increase, wispy gray bull pines appear on the hillsides, along with the showy white wands of California buckeye.

At 4,000 to 6,000 feet, a mixed coniferous forest of ponderosa pine, Douglas fir, and incense cedar flourishes, along with live oaks, deciduous black oaks, and maples. Warm, moist pockets support three separate groves of giant sequoias. Yosemite Valley, at about 4,000 feet, is at its finest in May and June. Waterfalls pour over the cliffs, and dogwoods and azaleas bloom along the streams. Mule deer, black bears, and several kinds of ground squirrels are active in spring, summer, and fall, along with a great variety of birds.

Lodgepole pine and red fir dominate at 6,500 to 8,000 feet. This is the zone of heaviest snowfall in winter. Moisture from the Pacific Ocean is wrung from the air and piled up here in deep snowdrifts that remain well into July. Forests are dark and deep with fairly open, bare floors because little sunlight reaches the ground. Yet odd little parasitic and saprophytic plants, including several kinds of orchids, thrive here, nourished by fungi and decaying material in the soil.

▶ **Whenever you pause beside a stream or a waterfall, watch for a little gray-brown bird whizzing along above the water. Then watch as it stops, perches on a streamside rock, and performs a vigorous series of squats, then walks right into and under the water as if it weren't there at all and begins to forage for aquatic organisms on the bottom. This is the American dipper, or water ouzel, our only aquatic songbird. It's John Muir's (and probably everybody's) favorite.**

The subalpine zone, from 8,000 to 10,000 feet, is considered by some to be the beginning of the true High Sierra. The landscape is more open and rocky, and the views are the finest. The sky is intensely blue because the air is thinner. Graceful mountain hemlocks stand tall at the lower end of this zone, but the lodgepole and whitebark pines near timberline are often gnarled and stunted, forced to hunker down to avoid howling winter winds. Belding ground squirrels and marmots whistle in the meadows, and showy black, white, and gray Clark's nutcrackers squawk among the trees.

The region of high peaks and passes above timberline is true arctic-alpine country. The temperature is low, winds high, and the growing season short, so plants keep their heads low. Most of the alpine wildflowers are perennials that wait underground for the few short weeks of sunshine and freedom from snow. Beginning roughly in mid-July and continuing through August, they burst forth to carpet the high meadows and decorate the rock crannies with masses of color. Across the late-lying snowfields, rosy finches chase insects that have been blown upward from below. Pikas scurry among the rock piles, gathering food to see them through the winter.

Then at the crest, all at once, the mountains fall away to the Great Basin. On the steep eastern slope, mountain and desert species mix together. Sagebrush and piñon pines appear. The very rock is different on the eastern side of the crest. Ancient red and white metamorphics remain above the much younger granite that underlies most of Yosemite. Many points along the crest reveal stupendous views of Mono Lake, the Owens Valley, and the White Mountains.

Geology

Yosemite occupies the central part of the Sierra Nevada, a 400-mile-long active dynamic classroom of geologic forces and features. The range was formed by the collision of vast plates of the earth's crust, lifting what had once been seafloor and offshore volcanic islands to become mountain peaks. Roughly 150 million years ago, huge globs of molten material called magma from beneath the earth's crust forced their way toward the surface, cooking the surrounding and overlying seafloor sediments to a new kind of rock known as metamorphic. Most of the molten material cooled and solidified beneath the surface to become granitic rock. Then, about 80 million years ago, mountain building ended for a time. For millennia rain, wind, and weather washed away almost all of the overlying ancient seafloor to reveal the gray granite that gives Yosemite its distinctive appearance today. A few remnants of the old metamorphic rock can still be seen in a narrow belt low in the western foothills and in another high on the Sierra crest, but more than 95 percent of the Sierra Nevada is granite.

About 25 million years ago, the range began to rise again, this time as a result of movement on the famous San Andreas Fault. North of Yosemite volcanoes erupted, blanketing the land in lava and ash. The entire range broke apart along its eastern border, the Sierra crest thrusting upward, the Owens Valley dropping down, so that the current range slopes gradually upward from west to east, until it reaches the crest, then drops away in a vertical cliff. Eventually the mountains gained enough height to block the flow of the moist winds that blow from the Pacific, which dropped their loads of rain and snow on the western flank of the range, cutting rivers and streams. The sediment washed away, filling the great central valley of California with rich and productive soil. The land to the east, now deprived of water, became desert.

The movement of ice applied the finishing touches to Yosemite's scenery. About 2 million to 3 million years ago, the climate of the earth cooled just a bit. Enormous ice caps formed over the poles and spread outward. While they did not reach Yosemite, the snows that did fall accumulated to great depths, then compressed to ice. The ice, under its own weight, began to flow down the previously cut stream courses, gouging them wider and deeper, scraping and polishing their bottoms and sides, sharpening the mountaintops into spires and horns, forming knife-edged ridges called arêtes and amphitheaters called cirques. The ice dug out basins in the rock, and when it melted it left thousands of alpine and subalpine lakes, many of which over time filled in with silt to become flower-filled mountain meadows. The glaciers in Yosemite today are not remnants of the original ice. The global climate has warmed and cooled in cycles since then, and the glaciers have melted and re-formed in response. The current glaciers are only a few hundred years old, but they lie in the hollows created by their larger predecessors, and the weather processes that created them are still at work. The mountain-building processes are at work too. The mountains are still being steadily, though not smoothly, uplifted. The Sierra is alive and growing. All along the eastern slope, hot springs steam and bubble along numerous faults, and earthquakes rattle local residents. As recently as 1872, an earthquake struck the Sierra to the south of Yosemite, lifting the mountains 15 to 20 feet in that area and devastating the small town of Lone Pine.

In Yosemite we can see the evidence of more than 200 million years of geologic history, and, as the mountains build and erode away, witness the process as it happens.

History

The southern Sierra Miwok people, who hunted, fished, and gathered a rich variety of plant materials, especially acorns, inhabited Yosemite for more than 800 years. They conducted trade with the Piute from the east side of the mountains for obsidian for arrowheads, salt, and various foods. Both made beautiful baskets.

Yosemite was first seen by outsiders in 1851 when the Mariposa battalion chased a band of Indians led by Chief Tenaya into the valley. Shortly thereafter the native people were forced to leave their villages in the area. By 1855 the first tourists had arrived, followed by the first homesteaders. Stagecoach routes, then railroads, were built to reach the valley. Sheep and cattle were turned into the meadows to graze and trample the grasses, and loggers began to cut the trees. Fortunately, a few farsighted individuals recognized the need for protection and set in motion the appropriate political machinery that led to President Abraham Lincoln's signing the bill that placed Yosemite Valley and the Mariposa Grove under the protection of the state of California. In 1868 the legendary John Muir arrived in Yosemite and led the movement for federal protection.

Yosemite National Park was created in 1890. All parks were patrolled by the US Cavalry until 1916 when their function was taken over by the National Park Service. Many trails and other facilities were constructed or expanded by federal agencies

Yosemite's meadows burst into bloom in spring and early summer.

This tame chicken-size bird is often seen from the trail.

The dipper was John Muir's favorite and our only aquatic songbird. SANDY STEINMAN

like the Works Progress Administration (WPA) and the Civilian Conservation Corps (CCC) during the Great Depression of the 1930s. After World War II people and cars poured into the park in ever-increasing numbers. Now Yosemite gets 4 million visitors each year, forcing the National Park Service to walk a tightrope between two somewhat contradictory mandates. It must "conserve the scenery and the natural and historic objects and the wildlife therein" and it must "provide for the enjoyment of the same in such manner and by such means as will leave them unimpaired for the enjoyment of future generations."

Providing access to the parks and accommodations within so that everyone can enjoy them without disrupting and changing them forever is an ongoing challenge. Roads, trails, campgrounds, other lodging, emergency services, administration, and sources of supply, no matter how carefully planned and constructed, inevitably make an impact on the natural environment.

Leave No Trace

While the primary aim of this book is to encourage you to experience and appreciate Yosemite's waterfalls up close and on foot, please keep in mind the fact that *Yosemite is not a theme park*.

Each of us must accept personal responsibility for our impact on the land, especially in the backcountry. Hikers can do their part by respecting park rules and practicing Leave No Trace principles (www.LNT.org).

Here are a few hints not only for protecting you from possible or perceived hazards in the wilderness but for protecting the wilderness from *you*.

Hiking on trails leaves the least impact on the land. To prevent damage to the trails themselves, do not shortcut switchbacks. Trails are built to retard erosion as well as create a more comfortable grade for gaining and losing elevation. When the trail is wet or muddy, try to avoid walking alongside it, trampling vegetation, and wearing a parallel trail. Many of Yosemite's meadows are scarred by a series of wide parallel ruts across the landscape that look like the work of vehicles. On the other hand, if you must cross a meadow with no conspicuous pathway and are part of a group, spread out so that you do not create a new rut by numerous feet passing over the same route.

Don't litter. *Cigarette butts and orange peels are litter!* Take only pictures, leave only footprints.

For Backpackers

Selecting a Campsite

Maximum group size for overnight trips is fifteen people (with a few exceptions). Camping is prohibited within 4 trail miles of Yosemite Valley, Hetch Hetchy Reservoir, Wawona, Glacier Point, and Tuolumne Meadows, and within 1 mile of any road. Otherwise you may camp anywhere you choose in the Yosemite wilderness as long as you observe a few restrictions designed to reduce your impact on the land and on other campers. Choose a site at least 100 feet from water and, whenever possible, 100 feet from the trail, or at least out of sight of passersby. Pitch your tent or spread your tarp on sandy ground or pine duff, never on growing vegetation. In the afternoon sunshine green meadows are deceptively inviting, but they are cold, damp, and buggy at night. Use an established campsite—one that has been used before—and do not modify the area in any way by digging trenches around tents, building new fire rings, or breaking limbs off trees.

Campfires

Campfires are prohibited above 9,600 feet in Yosemite and are discouraged even at lower elevations. If you must have a fire, keep it small and cozy, and take firewood that is dead and lying on the ground. Do not remove branches from standing dead trees. They provide homes for dozens of different creatures and are important parts of the ecosystem. High-elevation fires are proscribed not because of wildfire danger primarily, but because the 9,600-foot mark is the average timberline elevation in Yosemite, where vegetation grows slowly and the few trees that manage to hang on to life near timberline are evergreens that do not drop much organic material on the ground. The soil needs protection from the compaction that litter on the forest floor supplies, especially where people are moving around and pitching tents. Compaction prevents the soil from absorbing vital water and oxygen and removes the source of organic material that is returned to the soil as it decomposes.

Backpacking stoves are so light and efficient, and modern fabrics so warm, that fires are no longer needed for cooking or for warmth but for social atmosphere alone. As attractive as going "back to nature" seems, there are too many of us now and too little truly wild nature left to afford an extravagant campfire. Keep it small if you must have it, and of course, make sure it is completely out when you leave.

Housekeeping

There is one simple rule for good housekeeping in the wilderness: Do not put anything in the water. That includes soap, food scraps, and fish guts. Biodegradable soap is not the answer. To biodegrade means to decompose, that is, to rot. Biodegradable soap might not poison organisms in the water but it does encourage the growth of bacteria that can upset the chemical balance of the water to the detriment of the organisms that live in it. Hot water and a little sand do fine for washing dishes, but if you must use soap, wash and rinse everything at least 100 feet from any water source. The same goes for your own body. A refreshing swim in a mountain pond won't do any damage (though layers of sunblock and mosquito repellent don't do much good either), and you can surely survive a few days in the wilderness without contracting some dread disease if you don't use soap. But if you feel you must, wash and rinse at least 100 feet away from the shore.

Keep your camp or picnic site clean of crumbs and other edibles and pack out leftovers. At popular sites jays, squirrels, mice, and marmots have come to expect human food scraps, and have acquired bad habits like snatching food from your hand or chewing holes in your pack or tent to investigate appetizing smells.

Human waste disposal is one of the most difficult problems in the backcountry. There are simply too many of us concentrated in too few areas to avoid having a serious impact. The park service has constructed solar composting toilets at the most popular campsites in the park and encourages you to use them. Otherwise, find a spot 200 feet from water where there is some organic material on the ground, dig a hole about 6 inches deep, then cover everything.

Take extra plastic bags along and pack out your toilet paper. A teaspoon of powdered bleach in the plastic bag will prevent any odors. Do not bury it. It may be dug up again by animals and takes many years to decompose underground. Burning toilet paper is no longer recommended since the practice has started more than one serious fire.

For Your Safety

On the Trail

Hiking on trails leaves the least impact on the land, and they are the safest routes to travel by far, so all the hikes in this book follow established trails. To prevent damage to the trails and injury to yourself, do not shortcut switchbacks. They have been built to retard erosion as well as create a safer and more comfortable grade for gaining and losing elevation.

Stream Crossings

This is one wilderness hazard that is not exaggerated. Unlike imagined threats from wildlife, there have been many fatalities from drowning in Yosemite, almost all resulting from people trying to cross streams that are too deep, too cold, too swift. The leading cause of accidental death in Yosemite next to traffic accidents is drowning, and it is the leading cause of accidental death in the wilderness. Most of the larger streams have sturdy bridges across them, but in exceptionally wet years, some of these get washed away.

Be sure to research trail conditions in advance if your route involves a major river crossing. Waterfall photographers are vulnerable, especially when looking for the perfect angle from the middle of the stream. More frequently it is the smaller creeks swollen with snowmelt early in the year that are most

▶ **Your phone is fine for taking pictures, but there are very few locations in Yosemite with cell service.**

dangerous, and of course, this is when waterfalls are at their finest. Some have rock or log crossings that must be managed with great care. A stout stick is a great stabilizer if you don't have hiking poles. Be sure to plant it upstream so that rushing water does not grab it and pull it out from under you. Unbuckle your pack straps so that if you should fall in, you can free yourself from being dragged and held underwater. If you decide to wade, always overestimate the depth and the strength of the current. Sierra streams are so clear that they are usually deeper and swifter than they seem. Do not wade through water higher than your knees. The recommended method is to remove your socks and cross in your boots, which will give you temporary protection against the numbing cold and more stability on underwater obstacles. Do not try to cross barefooted. The widest spot is usually the shallowest, slowest, and safest. If you are not sure whether you can cross safely, turn around.

Losing the Trail

Yosemite trails are much better marked and maintained than those you will find in most wilderness areas. Still, some are used more regularly than others and are easier

Hikers must use great caution crossing streams at high water.

to follow. High water, avalanches, rockslides, and fast-growing meadow vegetation can obscure a clear trail in a single season. Watch for trail blazes on the trees, made by cutting away the outer bark, usually in simple geometric shapes approximately at eye level. In open rocky places, watch for cairns—piles of rock also known as ducks—that indicate the presence of a trail. Stay alert for sawed logs, metal tags, sometimes even plastic strips. If you become confused on the trail, go back to a point where you were absolutely certain of your location, and start over. If you feel you are hopelessly lost, stay put and wait for help.

Bears

All of Yosemite's bears are black bears, regardless of their color. The grizzly, the California state mammal, is now extinct in California. Black bears are neither as unpredictable nor as aggressive as grizzlies. No human has ever been killed by a black bear in Yosemite, but there have been injuries and property damage, and many vacations have been spoiled.

The fault is not with the bears. For many years Yosemite bears were fed scraps from local hotels, to the delight of tourists who came to watch the evening show. When the practice was discontinued, bears resorted to raiding garbage containers all over the park. When bear-resistant garbage containers were installed, bears mastered the art of opening ice chests in campgrounds, and when bear-proof boxes were installed in campgrounds, bears moved into the backcountry to feast on freeze-dried

▶ **Deer have caused more injuries than bears in Yosemite, including two deaths. People are more likely to approach or try to feed a deer and risk being sliced by sharp hooves when the animal is startled.**

backpack cuisine. At the same time they discovered what culinary delights are to be found in vehicles left in parking lots. The National Park Service had tried tagging, relocating, and even killing "problem" bears to no avail. Current and more effective park policy has shifted to change the behavior of the humans instead of the bears.

Use the bear-proof boxes located in parking lots and at trailheads. Rangers patrol regularly to make sure that no food or food containers have been left in parked cars. Parking lot "incidents" have now been dramatically reduced. Do not assume that if food is sealed in plastic or foil and has not been opened, or if it has been stowed in your trunk, a bear can't smell it.

The use of bear canisters is now required for overnight stays anywhere in the wilderness, and counterbalancing food from trees is no longer permitted. The canisters are not perfect; they are bulky, weigh 2 to 3 pounds, hold only a few days' food, and cost nearly $75 or more, but bears (usually) can't get into them. You can rent one from several different locations in Yosemite for up to two weeks for a small fee. The National Park Service considers proper food storage to be your responsibility. Don't expect sympathy if you lose your food. You are liable for a fine for not storing it properly.

If you should encounter a bear, or vice versa, in a public place or in a campground, adopt some loud and aggressive human behavior. Black bears are naturally afraid of people and will most likely change course to avoid you if you encounter one along the trail. Make enough noise for the bear to become aware of your presence. "Bear bells" are not loud enough to be effective or to frighten a bear, and pepper spray is illegal in Yosemite. (By the way, it is legal to carry a firearm here, but it is not legal to fire one.) Bears become dangerous when they lose their fear of people as they are likely to do when fed. Do not try to touch or feed a bear or to reclaim food a bear has already taken from you.

Other Animals

Mountain lions have been spotted in Yosemite, but they are very shy, and attacks are extremely rare. If you should encounter one, do not run or you might be mistaken for prey. Hold your ground, wave your arms to make yourself appear larger, and shout. Then congratulate yourself on being given the gift of a glimpse of a beautiful animal in its native habitat.

You'll find rattlesnake habitat at lower elevation where there is plenty of brush to provide cover for small animals like rabbits, squirrels, and mice. Rattlers are most active at dawn and dusk and blend beautifully with their surroundings. They prefer to

Drowning is the leading cause of accidental death in the wilderness. Marta Kis ▶

save their venom for catching their prey and do not strike at people unless they feel threatened. Stay alert and watch your step. The chances of being bitten are extremely slim, and snakebites are rarely fatal.

Do not feed the freeloading ground squirrels. Human food will not provide the nutrition they need to sustain them through the cold winter. Furthermore, they have become too tame and have lost most of their fear of people, but they may bite if startled. If you are bitten, you will need a tetanus shot. Also be aware that ground squirrels do carry plague.

The Bare Minimum Gear You Need to Carry on a Day Hike

Take extra plastic bags along and pack out your toilet paper. Do not burn or bury it.

Next to an extra toilet-paper bag, the most important items every hiker should carry on an expedition of even a couple of hours are:

- Extra sweater or jacket and any kind of rain protection, even a plastic trash bag. Mountain weather can and does change fast. High-country temperatures have been known to drop 60 degrees and a blue sky turn to dark gray with cold wind and icy hail in an hour or two.
- Sturdy hiking shoes or boots. Trails can be rough, rocky, and slippery.
- Plenty of water or some means of purification, whether tablets or filter.
- Sun protection, lip balm, cap, sunglasses.
- Basic first aid.
- A whistle.
- Insect repellent.
- Headlamp or small flashlight.
- Make sure you know where you are going. Use your map. A topo map and compass are advised, of course, if you know how to use them. A GPS is fun to use, but do not depend on electronic gadgets.

Trail Finder

Hike #	Hike Name	Tall	Secluded	Swimming	For Children	Backpackers	Least effort/ Short Distance	Year Round	Ephemeral
	YOSEMITE VALLEY WATERFALLS								
1	Vernal Fall Bridge				●			●	
2	Top of Nevada Fall via John Muir Trail	●						●	
3	Top of Vernal and Nevada Fall via the Mist Trail	●						●	
4	Silver Apron							●	
5	Lower Yosemite Falls	●			●		●		
6	Upper Yosemite Falls from Yosemite Valley	●							
7	Yosemite Falls from Tioga Road	●				●			
8	Bridalveil Fall				●		●	●	
9	Silver Strand Fall						●		●
10	Ribbon Fall	●			●		●		●
11	Cascade Creek Falls	●			●		●		

Hike #	Hike Name	Tall	Secluded	Swimming	For Children	Backpackers	Least effort/ Short Distance	Year Round	Ephemeral
12	Upper Cascade Creek Cascades	●		●	●	●			
13	Sentinel Fall	●			●		●		
14	Illilouette Fall	●		●	●			●	
15	Staircase Fall				●		●		●
16	Lehamite Fall	●	●		●		●		●
17	Upper Snow Creek Falls		●			●			
18	Horsetail Fall				●		●		●
19	Royal Arch Cascade				●		●		●
20	Basket Dome Fall		●		●				●
	WATERFALLS OF THE WESTERN FOOTHILLS								
21	Red Rock Falls			●	●		●		
22	Corlieu Falls			●	●				

Hike #	Hike Name	Tall	Secluded	Swimming	For Children	Backpackers	Least effort/ Short Distance	Year Round	Ephemeral
23	Foresta Falls								
24	Little Nellie Falls		•	•		•			
25	Preston Falls		•	•		•			
	WAWONA-AREA FALLS								
26	Alder Creek Falls		•						
27	Chilnualna Falls	•				•			
	WATERFALLS IN THE HEART OF THE PARK								
28	Merced River Falls					•		•	
29	Bunnell Cascade			•		•		•	
30	Merced Lake Cascades			•		•		•	
31	Fletcher Creek Cascades					•		•	
32	Vogelsang Cascades				•	•			

Hike #	Hike Name	Tall	Secluded	Swimming	For Children	Backpackers	Least effort/ Short Distance	Year Round	Ephemeral
	WATERFALLS OF THE TUOLUMNE MEADOWS REGION								
33	Rafferty Creek Falls								
34	Kuna Falls	•	•	•	•	•			
35	Ireland Lake Falls	•							
36	Lyell Fork Cascades			•	•			•	
37	Dana Fork Cascades			•	•		•	•	
38	Young Lakes Falls					•			
	HETCH HETCHY WATERFALLS								
39	Carlon Falls				•		•		
40	Tueeulala Falls								•
41	Wapama Falls	•							•
42	Rancheria Falls			•		•		•	
43	Lake Vernon Cascade					•		•	

Hike #	Hike Name	Tall	Secluded	Swimming	For Children	Backpackers	Least effort/ Short Distance	Year Round	Ephemeral
	GRAND CANYON OF THE TUOLUMNE RIVER WATERFALLS								
44	Tuolumne Falls and the White Cascade					•		•	
45	Waterwheel Falls via LeConte and California Falls					•		•	
46	The Grand Canyon of the Tuolumne					•		•	
	WATERFALLS OF THE SIERRA CREST								
47	Mill Creek Falls								
48	Parker Pass Falls								
49	Ellery Lake Falls	•				•	•	•	
50	West Lake Falls	•	•	•		•			
51	Cooney Lake Falls								•

Map Legend

Municipal

395 US Highway

120 State Road

Local/County Road

Unpaved Road

Leader Line

Trails

Featured Trail

Trail or Fire Road

Water Features

Body of Water

River/Creek

Intermittent Stream

Spring

Rapids

Waterfall

Symbols

Bridge

Building/Point of Interest

Campground

Gate

Hike Arrow

Inn/Lodging

Parking

Pass/Gap

Peak/Elevation

Picnic Area

Scenic View

Town

To Text

Trailhead

Visitor/Information Center

Land Management

National Park/Forest

Yosemite Valley Waterfalls

When most people think of Yosemite National Park, it's Yosemite Valley alone that comes to mind. Some are surprised to discover that Yosemite Valley occupies only a small, fairly flat-bottomed finger of land roughly a mile wide and 7 miles long, extending into the heart of a 1,200-square-mile expanse of national park wilderness with glaciers and peaks higher than 13,000 feet.

Still, you will find more waterfalls described in this section of the book than in any other, partly because there are so many big (and world-famous) falls concentrated here. In fact, Yosemite Valley probably has a greater number of significant waterfalls in an area of comparable size than anywhere else in the world. The biggest ones, Yosemite Falls and Ribbon Fall, are usually included in the several (informal) international lists of North America's and even the world's ten highest falls. (There is no official international listing.) Spectacular as these waterfalls are by themselves, they are all set in the grandest, most exquisitely beautiful landscape on earth.

The valley's falls are (for better or for worse) easily accessible too. The park is close to large population centers and attracts visitors from all over the world so you can expect plenty of company. It doesn't require a difficult or dangerous expedition to some remote corner of the globe . . . or even a multiday excursion to a remote corner of the park, as some of the falls in the following sections do. Easy to moderate day hikes on good trails will take you to most of them.

The timing of your visit to Yosemite Valley is especially important if you are a waterfall lover. Some of its falls flow year-round, and most are at their best from early spring to early summer. Others, even the biggest, may be completely dry by mid-August. The valley floor, at 4,000 feet, can be hot and dry in summer. In fact, 95 percent of the park's precipitation occurs in winter in the form of snow. Once the snowpack that has accumulated in the high country over the winter has melted and poured down the canyons, over the cliffs, into the rivers, and on to the Central Valley of California, it's gone until next year.

For a more enjoyable Yosemite Valley experience, bring an alarm clock and get up early in the morning even if it is a vacation. Yosemite nowadays receives about 5

million visitors each year, most of whom concentrate their activities in the 7 square miles of Yosemite Valley, and most come in spring and summer. The National Park Service does its best to accommodate the crowds and to protect the environment with free shuttle buses and controlled traffic flow, but gridlock has become a regular occurrence on valley roads in recent years, and the day-use parking lots are often full by 10 a.m. Get up early, park your car during your visit, and walk, rent a bicycle, or ride the free shuttle buses that go almost everywhere. Morning is the most pleasant time to be out and about anyway; birds and animals are more active then, and after-noons can be hot. Some waterfalls are better to view and photograph later in the day depending on the angle of the sun, of course, so you might want to plan ahead.

Reminder: There is no gas available in Yosemite Valley.

◀ *Vernal and Nevada Falls flow into Yosemite Valley down the Giant Staircase.*

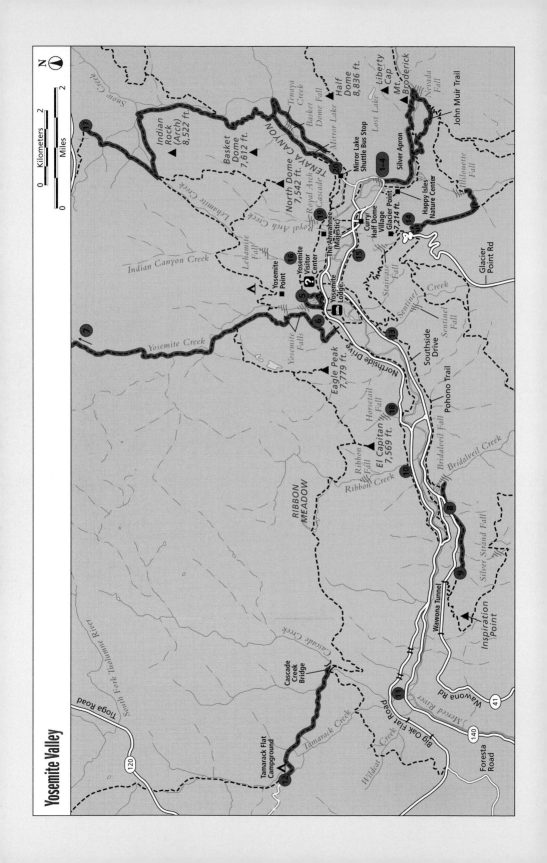

1 Vernal Fall Bridge

This is probably the most popular short hike in Yosemite. Here the Merced, one of the two major rivers in the park, plunges down the steps of the Giant Staircase between almost vertical cliffs in two sections, set off from each other at an angle created by joints in the granitic rock. You can't see the upper fall, Nevada, from here because of the angle, but the lower fall, Vernal, is a wonder in itself, perfectly framed for photos, especially toward afternoon. You can (and should) see the entire Giant Stairway best from Glacier Point. Unlike so many of Yosemite's waterfalls, this one flows all year and is exciting even at low water since it drains an area of more than 100 square miles. Along the way you get bonus views of two more of Yosemite's finest falls: the iconic Yosemite Falls and Illilouette Fall, big and beautiful, but often overlooked tucked away in its side canyon.

Height of fall: 317 feet
Start: Happy Isles
Distance: 1.6 miles out and back
Hiking time: 1–1.5 hours
Elevation change: 400 feet
Difficulty: Easy
Seasons: The fall flows all year but is most spectacular May through early July. Beyond the lower Vernal Fall Bridge, trails become icy and may be closed in winter.

Nearest facilities: Toilets and water at the trailhead and at the Vernal Fall Bridge
Permits: None
Maps: Half Dome USGS quad
Special considerations: Expect lots of company. Yosemite's trails are usually on natural surfaces, but this one gets so much traffic, it's paved. The secret to happy hiking here: Hit the trail early, before 8 a.m. if possible.

Finding the trailhead: Take the free shuttle bus to Happy Isles (stop 16), or park in the hikers' lot east of Half Dome (Curry) Village, turn right (east) at the far end of the lot, and follow the well-marked path to Happy Isles. This will add a mile round-trip to your hike. Continue on the paved road over the Happy Isles Bridge, then turn right (south) following the river upstream to the big sign on the left that marks the beginning of the John Muir Trail. Trailhead GPS: N37 43.55' / W119 33.35'

The Hike

Leave the wide path that runs southward along the Merced River and turn left up the narrower trail into the forest, where in a few feet you will find a big sign marking the beginning of the John Muir Trail with mileages all the way to Mount Whitney. The route climbs through black oak and pine forest among enormous lichen-draped boulders along the southeast bank of the Merced. A little spring trickles out of the rocks a few hundred yards up on your left. (**Note:** Don't drink the water here without purifying it.) The trail steepens gradually as you climb, but you will want to stop frequently to enjoy the roaring river below through openings in the trees.

Vernal Fall flows over the bottom step of the Giant Staircase.

▶ **Nevada means "snowy." Vernal means "springtime." The Merced River was named El Rio de Nuestra Senora de la Merced (The River of Our Lady of Mercy), which was discovered around the feast day of Our Lady of Mercy in 1806 by Gabriel Moraga, who was part of a Spanish expedition seeking locations to establish missions in California.**

After about 0.4 mile look across the Merced to your right. Tucked into Illilouette Gorge, Illilouette Fall pours 370 feet down the Panorama Cliff to meet the Merced River. It's a big, beautiful waterfall, but you might miss it if you're toiling up the path looking at your feet. Stop now and then to glance behind you to find that Upper Yosemite Falls is visible too.

The trail makes a short descent to the bridge at 0.8 mile, where dozens of visitors will be taking photos or gazing in delight at 317-foot Vernal Fall upstream from the far end of the bridge. There are restrooms nearby, a water fountain, and dozens of freeloading ground squirrels. For their health and your safety, do not feed them. When you are ready, return the way you came.

Miles and Directions

0.0 John Muir Trailhead at Happy Isles
0.4 View of Illilouette Fall to the right
0.8 Vernal Fall Bridge
1.6 Arrive back at the trailhead

2 Top of Nevada Fall via John Muir Trail

This is not the shortest but is definitely the safest and easiest route up the Giant Stairway to the top of Nevada Fall. It's your chance to sample the first few miles of the famous John Muir Trail and to enjoy one wondrous view after another. You also get to take in four major waterfalls in one hike. At the top, your first cautious glance over the roaring 594-foot fall is as good as a thrill ride. You can combine this hike with the Mist Trail route, ascending by one trail, descending by the other. The Muir Trail route is the recommended route for backpackers because it is wider, less slippery, and allows you to keep your gear dry.

Height of fall: 594 feet
Start: John Muir Trailhead at Happy Isles
Distance: 7.0 miles out and back
Hiking time: 3 hours to all day
Elevation change: 2,000 feet
Difficulty: Moderate
Seasons: Spring, summer, and fall, May and June for the most spectacular show and rainbows. Sections are closed in winter.
Nearest facilities: Toilets and water at Happy Isles and Vernal Fall Bridge. There are toilets 0.2 mile south of the top of Nevada Fall, but no potable water.

Permits: None
Maps: USGS Half Dome quad
Special considerations: Please take the warning signs very seriously and stay out of the river. The water upstream is tempting and there are inviting little pools that beckon after your hot climb, but even wading can be lethal in early season. Do not underestimate the force of the river. Somebody is swept downstream and over the falls almost every year. Nobody survives.

Finding the trailhead: Take the free shuttle bus to Happy Isles (stop 16), or park in the hikers' lot east of Half Dome (Curry) Village, turn right (east) at the far end of the lot, and follow the well-marked path to Happy Isles. This will add a mile round-trip to your hike. Continue on the paved road over the Happy Isles Bridge, then turn right, following the river upstream to the big sign on the left that marks the beginning of the John Muir Trail. Trailhead GPS: N37 33.55' / W119 33.35'

The Hike

The John Muir Trail sign shows mileage to various points all the way to trail's end at Mount Whitney, about 211 miles to the south. You will have lots of company on this walk because it's the beginning of a famous trail and is a major route out of the valley to the high country. The first part of it gets so much traffic that it has been paved, but don't let that deter you. It's popular for good reason.

The trail climbs gently through black oak and pine forest among enormous lichen-draped boulders up along the north bank of the Merced. A little spring trickles out of the rocks a few hundred yards up on your left. (**Note:** Don't drink the

Nevada Fall tumbles over the first step of the Giant Staircase.

water here without purifying it.) The trail steepens gradually as you climb, but you'll want to stop frequently anyway to enjoy the roaring river through openings in the trees. In about a half mile, across the Merced canyon to your right and tucked back up in Illilouette Gorge, Illilouette Fall pours 370 feet down the Panorama Cliff to meet the Merced River. It is a big waterfall but most people miss it. If you stop now and then to glance behind you, you will find that Upper Yosemite Falls is visible too.

The trail suddenly descends to the bridge at 0.8 mile, where dozens of visitors will be taking photos or gazing in delight at 317-foot Vernal Fall upstream. There are restrooms, a water fountain, and dozens of freeloading, usually overweight ground squirrels near the bridge. For their health and your safety, do not feed them.

Cross the bridge to the south side of the river and turn left (upstream). At 1.1 mile the Mist Trail stays to the left. Your route turns right on the John Muir Trail and ascends on well-graded switchbacks through shady mixed conifer forest until you round a corner to Clark Point at mile 2.1. Here, one of the most spectacular of Yosemite's many overlooks will stop you in your tracks as Nevada Fall thunders down the canyon straight ahead in classic postcard style. The rounded shape behind and just to the left of Liberty Cap (itself just to the left of the fall) is the back side of Half Dome.

From Clark Point a steep rocky trail heads downhill to the left to connect with the Mist Trail, but you turn right, climb a few more switchbacks, then pass through a cut in the side of the cliff beneath a weeping rock overhang that drizzles water onto the trail. Delicate ferns, columbines, and tiny white orchids are tucked into the

Nevada Fall is just around the corner. ▶

Clark Point on the John Muir Trail first reveals Nevada Fall.

cracks. Begin to lose a little elevation, and at mile 3.1 pass through an open gate at a junction with the Panorama Trail. Continue left through a shady little gully where water sometimes pools deeply enough to slosh over the tops of your boots, then round a corner to emerge onto a sunny bench. A bridge passes over the Merced River, which runs through the middle of the bench, and the best views of the fall are not far beyond this. Nevada Fall crashes through an impossibly narrow notch and is visible all the way to the bottom, sometimes projecting a rainbow near the base. There are several great viewpoints for watching Nevada Fall where it shoots over the rim and explodes into foam and froth on the rocks almost 600 feet below. Stay behind protective railings and heed the warnings about wading or swimming above the falls, and don't forget to keep an eye on your lunch. The local squirrels and jays will make off with it if your attention wanders for too long.

Miles and Directions

0.0 John Muir Trailhead
0.8 Cross the Merced River on the bridge
1.1 Mist Trail junction; keep right
2.1 Clark Point; turn right again
3.1 Panorama Trail junction; keep left
3.5 Top of Nevada Fall
7.0 Arrive back at Happy Isles

3 Vernal and Nevada Falls from the Mist Trail

The Mist Trail is one of two routes that follow the Merced River up the Giant Stairway to the top of Vernal and Nevada Falls. It is surely one of the most beautiful and exciting hikes in Yosemite, but it is steep, narrow, exposed, and crowded. From May into July you are bound to be soaked by the spray from the falls but exhilarated by the climb and enchanted by the rainbows. It is strenuous but a great adventure if you are in good condition. It's not recommended for little kids, and backpackers are advised to use the alternate route, the John Muir Trail, for reasons of safety and to keep their gear dry, but many use it anyway. A wilderness experience, no. The most awe-inspiring experience you'll ever have? Definitely.

Height of Vernal Fall: 317 feet
Height of Nevada Fall: 594 feet
Start: Happy Isles
Distance: 5.4 miles out and back
Hiking time: 4 hours to all day
Elevation change: 2,000 feet
Difficulty: Strenuous
Seasons: Closed in winter
Nearest facilities: Toilets and water at Happy Isles and at the Vernal Fall Bridge. Toilets only at the top of Vernal Fall and at the top of Nevada Fall. Gas in Wawona or Crane Flat.
Permits: None
Maps: Half Dome

Special considerations: *Do not* swim or wade in the Emerald Pool at the top of Vernal Fall or in the Merced River above Nevada Fall, no matter how calm the water appears. The river's power is deceptive and the falls have claimed many lives. In spring and early summer, expect to be soaked by the spray from the falls. Take rain gear and be sure to protect your camera. The trail ascends on large, slippery stone steps and, except for one very short section, has no handrails. Don't try it with flip-flops, and take a dry shirt or sweater. It gets cold and windy up there.

Finding the trailhead: Take the free shuttle bus to Happy Isles (stop 16), or park in the hikers' lot east of Half Dome (Curry) Village, turn right (east) at the far end of the lot, and follow the well-marked path to Happy Isles. This will add a mile round-trip to your hike. Continue on the paved road over the Happy Isles Bridge, then turn right (south), following the river upstream to the big sign on the left that marks the beginning of the John Muir Trail. Trailhead GPS: N37 43.51' / W119 33.55'

The Hike

Leave the wide path that runs southward along the Merced River and turn left up the narrower trail into the forest, where in a few feet you will find a big sign marking the beginning of the John Muir Trail with mileages all the way to Mount Whitney. The route climbs through black oak and pine forest among enormous lichen-draped

The Mist Trail clings closely to the north shore of Nevada Fall.

The Mist Trail crosses the Merced River above Vernal Fall.

boulders along the southeast bank of the river. A little spring trickles out of the rocks a few hundred yards up on your left. (**Note:** Don't drink the water here without purifying it.) The trail steepens gradually as you climb. After about 0.4 mile look across the Merced to your right. Tucked into Illilouette Gorge, Illilouette Fall pours 370 feet down the Panorama Cliff to meet the Merced River. It's a big, beautiful waterfall, but you might miss it if you're toiling up the path looking at your feet. Stop now and then to glance behind you to find that Upper Yosemite Falls is visible too. The trail makes a short descent to the bridge at 0.8 mile, where dozens of visitors will be taking photos or gazing at 317-foot Vernal Fall upstream. (You won't see the fall until you are almost all the way across the bridge.) There are restrooms nearby, a water fountain, and dozens of freeloading ground squirrels. For their health and your safety, do not feed them.

After crossing the bridge to the south side, turn left (upstream). At 1.1 miles keep left where a sign says "Foot Trail Only, Top of Vernal Fall via Mist Trail." Get out your rain gear here. The trail climbs steeply through the spray on big wet stone blocks. The thunder of the falls is almost deafening in early season; morning sunlight through the spray has a diffuse mystical quality, and there's always a rainbow or two if the sun is shining. At the top of the fall, the Merced pauses to collect itself in the deceptively quiet Emerald Pool before flinging itself over the cliff. A long, slanting ramp called the Silver Apron tempts the sweaty hiker to ride this waterslide into the pool. *Don't do it!* In an instant you can be washed over the rim to the rocks 317 feet below. Above the Silver Apron, at 1.6 miles, cross another bridge over the Merced to a flat, where a hotel, La Casa Nevada, was opened in 1870 then destroyed by fire in

Hikers climb through rainbows on the way to the top of Vernal Fall.

1891. Begin climbing steeply again along the river's north shore amid more rumbling and spray. Another set of switchbacks brings you through a notch out onto a sunny bench above the fall at mile 2.7, where you will find a restroom and a junction with the John Muir Trail. Turn right (south) here to emerge onto an open bench at the top of the fall to rest and reward yourself for your effort in a perfect spot for sunbathing and picnicking. There are several great viewpoints for watching Nevada Fall where it shoots over the rim and explodes into foam and froth on the rocks almost 600 feet below. Stay behind protective railings and heed the warnings about wading or swimming above the falls, and don't forget to keep an eye on your lunch. The local squirrels and jays will make off with it if your attention wanders for too long.

From here you can return to Happy Isles the same way you came, down the Mist Trail, but the John Muir Trail is an easier and safer route going downhill and gives you a new and different set of spectacular views. You will wind up at Happy Isles, where you began.

Miles and Directions

0.0 Happy Isles

0.8 Vernal Fall Bridge; cross the bridge and turn left

1.1 Mist Trail junction; keep left

1.6 Top of Vernal Fall

2.7 Top of Nevada Fall

5.4 Arrive back at Happy Isles via Mist Trail (or 6.2 via John Muir Trail)

4 Silver Apron

Just above the knickpoint (the very spot at the top where the creek drops over the cliff edge) of Vernal Fall is the deceptively tranquil and inviting (at least after first snowmelt time) Emerald Pool. It is fed by the Merced's Diamond Cascade down a sloping slide called the Silver Apron. In May and June its roiling wild descent is exciting to watch, but in summer when the Merced isn't in such a hurry to reach Yosemite Valley, it appears to be just the right grade, the water just the right depth to take a wild ride down the slick rock into the Emerald Pool. Do not even think of doing this! The pool seems quiet on the surface, but the pull of the water is powerful enough to suck you over the lower edge and, after a short, bone-crushing rocky cascade, fling you over the top of Vernal Fall and down 317 feet. There have been fatalities here.

Height of fall: About 35 feet
Start: Happy Isles
Distance: 3.4 miles out and back
Hiking time: 2-3 hours
Elevation change: 1,000 feet
Difficulty: Moderate but steep

Seasons: Spring, summer, fall
Nearest facilities: Toilets, water at Happy Isles, Vernal Fall Bridge
Permits: None
Maps: Half Dome

Finding the trailhead: Take the free shuttle bus to Happy Isles (stop 16), or park in the hikers' lot east of Half Dome (Curry) Village, turn right (east) at the far end of the lot, and follow the well-marked path to Happy Isles. This will add a mile round-trip to your hike. Continue on the paved road over the Happy Isles Bridge, then turn right (south), following the river upstream to the big sign on the left that marks the beginning of the John Muir Trail. Trailhead GPS N37 43.51' / W119 33.35'

The Hike

Leave the wide path that runs southward along the Merced River and turn left up the narrower trail into the forest, where in a few feet you will find a big sign marking the beginning of the John Muir Trail with mileages all the way to Mount Whitney. The route climbs through black oak and pine forest among enormous lichen-draped boulders, passing a little spring that trickles out of the rocks a few hundred yards up. (**Note:** Don't drink the water here without purifying it.) The trail steepens gradually as you climb. After about 0.4 mile look across the Merced to your right. Tucked into Illilouette Gorge, Illilouette Fall pours 370 feet down the Panorama Cliff to meet the Merced River. It's a big, beautiful waterfall, but you might miss it if you're toiling up the path looking at your feet. Stop now and then to glance behind you to find that Upper Yosemite Falls is visible too. The trail makes a short descent to the bridge at 0.8 mile, where dozens of visitors will be taking pictures or gazing in delight at

The yellow-legged frog is disappearing from Yosemite.

317-foot Vernal Fall upstream. (You won't see the fall until you are almost all the way across the bridge.) There are restrooms nearby, a water fountain, and dozens of freeloading ground squirrels. For their health and your safety, do not feed them.

After crossing the bridge to the south side, turn left (upstream). The crowd will thin out a bit here. At 1.1 miles keep left where a sign says "Foot Trail Only, Top of Vernal Fall via Mist Trail." Get out your rain gear here.

The trail climbs steeply through the spray and the rainbows on big wet stone blocks. There is a short section with a handrail at the very narrowest stretch of the trail, but most of the time there is no protection from all the other people climbing or descending around you.

You emerge from almost underneath the Vernal Fall at mile 1.6 to a sloping rocky flat where a crowd of damp hikers are drying themselves and their clothes in the sunshine, or more rarely shivering and digging through packs for sweaters if it's cloudy and there is a breeze. Another group will be leaning against the guardrails staring at the crashing fall and admiring the rainbows. Now follow the trail a short distance uphill into a small grove of trees beside the deep blue-green Emerald Pool. Just above the pool is the shining Silver Apron. Early in the season there are a couple of small waterwheels a short distance upstream. To repeat: In middle to late season, the surface of the pool appears to be quiet and the slope of the Silver Apron seems

The tempting slide into the Emerald Pool from the Silver Apron can be fatal.

just perfect for a slide into the pool. Some hikers try it almost every year, and almost every year some of them die.

From here you can continue on up the Mist Trail or the John Muir Trail to Nevada Fall, or you can follow a connector trail up to the John Muir Trail to return to Happy Isles, or you can return the way you came, back down the lower Mist Trail.

Miles and Directions

0.0 Happy Isles

0.8 Bridge below Vernal Fall

1.1 Junction of the John Muir and Mist Trails; keep left alongside the Merced

1.6 Top of Vernal Fall; continue uphill along the Merced

1.7 Base of the Silver Apron

3.4 Arrive back at Happy Isles

5 Lower Yosemite Falls

Yosemite Falls (along with Half Dome) is the image that comes to mind when people all over the world think of Yosemite. The triple-tiered cataract is visible from all over Yosemite Valley and much of the valley rim, where it is sometimes audible as well. This short hike gives you the most complete, head-on, top-to-bottom encounter with the famous falls and takes you so close that you can feel the spray.

This is Yosemite's (and North America's) highest waterfall, at 2,425 feet, and is said by some to be second highest the world, and by others, the fifth highest. (Angel Falls in Venezuela is the highest.) It doesn't descend the entire 2,425 feet in one free fall but begins as an upper fall of 1,430 feet, continues as a less conspicuous but impressive 675-foot cascade, and meets the valley floor in a shorter fall of 320 feet.

It does not flow year-round, a fact that disappoints visitors who come to Yosemite in mid- to late August. The area of the north rim that Yosemite Creek drains is mostly bare glacially scoured rock with a thin cover of poorly developed soil that does not retain water. Once winter snow has melted and the meltwater has flowed over the impermeable granite of the rim, the falls are no more until the next rain or snow comes.

In winter Yosemite Falls puts on a new show when mist from the upper fall freezes and builds an enormous ice cone at its base that may become taller than 200 feet. Then, in May, on a full moon night, if you are very lucky indeed, you might get to witness the rare and ghostly "moonbow," an actual rainbow that appears in the spray after dark. (Be prepared to join a crowd of other hopeful photographers waiting on the bridge for a shot, and keep your camera dry.)

Height of falls: 2,425 feet all together. Upper fall 1,430 feet, middle 675 feet, lower 320 feet.
Start: Trailhead just west of shuttle bus stop 6 and the picnic area
Distance: 0.6-mile loop
Hiking time: 30 minutes to an hour
Elevation change: Minimal
Difficulty: Easy
Seasons: Spring and early summer. By late August the falls are usually dry until the first autumn rain or snow.
Nearest facilities: Toilets and water at the picnic area at the trailhead. Food and supplies available at Yosemite Lodge and Yosemite Village. Gas at Wawona and Crane Flat.
Permits: None
Maps: USGS Half Dome, and Yosemite Falls, but a map is not necessary
Special considerations: Timing is all-important. The falls are glorious in May and June, lovely in early July, usually completely dry by mid-August. Despite posted warnings, the big slippery boulders at the base of the fall are often crawling with people; accidents and injuries are frequent.

Finding the trailhead: Ride the Yosemite Valley shuttle from anywhere in the valley to stop 6, Yosemite Falls Trailhead. The nearest parking for your car is about a half-mile walk along the road west of Yosemite Lodge. Trailhead GPS: N37 44.46' / W119 35.48'

An easy trail leads hikers of all abilities to the best view of Yosemite Falls.

Yosemite Creek crashes onto giant boulders at the base of Yosemite Falls.

The Hike

For maximum visual impact, walk this loop clockwise. Follow the wide paved path to the left (west) of the picnic area as it winds almost imperceptibly uphill through ponderosa pine and incense cedar forest. At several points along the route are turnouts with interpretive panels about the human and natural history of the area that are worth pausing to read, and there are plenty of opportunities to photograph the falls. The crashing of the water becomes louder and louder and the trail curves to cross a bridge very close to the base of the falls. If spring snowmelt on the peaks above is under way, you're sure to be dampened by the spray. Beyond the bridge the trail follows the base of the cliff and then swings south behind some park employee housing. It winds past braided strands of the now-divided creek, curves again to parallel Northside Drive, and then returns to the starting point at the picnic area.

▶ A. L. Kroeber, an early ethnologist, recounts a legend of the Miwok people of Yosemite who said that the spirit of Yosemite Falls was called Poloti, who took the form of an evil wind. When a local woman went to Yosemite Creek to fetch water, her basket came up full of snakes every time she dipped it in. When she finally reached a pool at the base of the falls, the evil wind blew her in. (I know, I don't get it either.) Kroeber may have been confused or may have been deliberately misled. According to some of Yosemite's native people, such myths are the private property of their culture, are probably wildly, perhaps deliberately, distorted, and are not the business of foreign interlopers or for the entertainment of tourists.

Miles and Directions

0.0 Trailhead west of the Yosemite Falls shuttle stop and picnic area

0.2 Bridge at Yosemite Falls

0.6 Arrive back at the trailhead

6 Upper Yosemite Falls from Yosemite Valley

You can do this one as a steep up-and-back day hike or spend the night near the top of Yosemite Falls. Although the views back down into Yosemite Valley are exciting, you don't get to see more than a short section of the falls themselves until you're on top. If you go in springtime when snow is melting rapidly and Yosemite Creek is in flood, the experience of standing beside the very lip of the upper fall as it roars over the cliff is unforgettable and worth almost any amount of hard climbing.

Yosemite Falls, like others in the park, are at their finest and fullest in springtime and are still beautiful, though less powerful, in July, but by late August they are sometimes reduced to a trickle or are completely dry. The land drained by Yosemite Creek is mostly bare, glacially scoured rock with a thin cover of poorly developed soil that does not retain water. Once the winter snowpack has melted, water simply runs off the impermeable granite, pours over the rim of the valley, and the falls are no more until the next rain or snow comes in autumn. For comparison, Bridalveil Fall on the opposite side of the valley is broader and is underlain by deeper soil and denser vegetation that acts as a sponge to soak up and store meltwater from winter snow that it releases slowly throughout the summer.

Height of falls: 2,425 feet
Start: Upper Yosemite Falls Trailhead at Camp 4
Distance: 7.6 miles out and back
Hiking time: 4 hours to all day as a day hike, or overnight as a backpack
Elevation change: 2,630 feet
Difficulty: Strenuous
Seasons: Lake spring, early summer
Nearest facilities: Food, water, toilets, phones at Yosemite Lodge and Yosemite Village
Permits: None for a day hike, available for overnights in advance or from the wilderness center in Yosemite Village

Maps: USGS Half Dome and Yosemite Falls quads
Special considerations: This hike can be hot and dry by midsummer and there is no potable water, so take plenty with you or be prepared to purify the water from Yosemite Creek. By mid-August there may be so little water left in the creek that there is not much point in making the climb to the top of the falls. The upper part of the trail can be icy and dangerous in winter.

Finding the trailhead: Take the shuttle bus from anywhere in Yosemite Valley to Camp 4, shuttle stop 7. A sign in front points the way to the Upper Yosemite Falls Trailhead, marked by another, larger sign at the back of Camp 4 listing mileage and other information about the trail. Trailhead GPS: N37 44.34' / W119 36.11'

The Hike

Begin climbing immediately up rocky switchbacks, winding your way among house-size boulders shaded by canyon live oak, ponderosa pine, and incense cedar. Slowly,

Tattered rain clouds drift over the face of Yosemite Falls.

more and more of the valley floor comes into view through the trees until, at 1 mile, you reach an overlook protected by iron railings known as Columbia Rock, where you'll probably need a breather. The trail ascends a few soft, gravelly switchbacks, then descends for a short distance, crosses several little rivulets that support delicate moss and fern gardens growing among the rocks, rounds a corner, and suddenly reveals 1,430-foot Upper Yosemite Falls, booming like thunder early in the summer. Over the roar of the falls, listen for the sweet, descending notes of the song of the canyon wren. The trail now ascends very steep, rough stairsteps past the top of the lower falls and all of the middle falls (675 feet). Notice the trickles of water seeping out of the cracks between the layers of exfoliating (peeling) granite. Partway up the upper falls, the trail ducks behind a ridge, concealing the falls from view until you reach the top. Climb the sunny defile densely clothed in scrub oak, except where a huge pile of talus has spilled into the gully. Above the rock pile you can see a white scar on the cliff above where the darker, lichen-stained rock broke away in 1980 and killed three hikers. This part of the trail can be hot.

As you near the top of the gulch, firs, Jeffrey pines, and a refreshing springtime trickle make a rest at the Yosemite Creek junction at 3.6 miles welcome. Follow the right fork for a few yards, then follow signs to Yosemite Falls Overlook, through sculpted rocks and twisted Jeffrey pines, to an iron railing at 3.8 miles. Across the valley the upside-down bowl of Sentinel Dome rises alone and to the west of Glacier Point. Farther in the distance is Mount Starr King, also rounded and isolated from the surrounding ridges, and beyond that, beautiful Mount Clark and the Clark Range define the horizon.

The path now drops down a series of steep and sometimes slippery steps cut into the cliff to a platform protected by more iron railings. The roar, the drenching spray, and the dizzying drop over the falls are exhilarating but not for the faint of heart or the acrophobic.

(**Option:** For a different perspective, return to the main trail and turn right [southeast], continuing for about 250 feet to a footbridge that spans Yosemite Creek a few yards upstream from the brink.)

The view from Sentinel Dome reveals the surprising geologic history of Yosemite Falls.

▶ **Doesn't it seem like the water should be flowing down the gully that contains the trail you're walking up on? This becomes more striking from viewpoints across the valley. The upper falls should be tumbling down this deep gully rather than pouring through the smaller, narrower notch to the right. Geologists explain that early glacial advances deposited moraines that blocked the original course of Yosemite Creek thousands of years ago, deflecting its course into its current location.**

You can return the way you came, or if you are planning to spend the night, follow the left (west) side of the creek upstream for at least 0.25 mile to several good campsites. *(Note: Camping within 0.25 mile of the rim is prohibited.)*

Miles and Directions

0.0 Upper Yosemite Falls Trailhead
1.0 Columbia Rock lookout
3.6 Yosemite Creek junction; turn right
3.8 Yosemite Falls Overlook. Turn around to retrace your steps back to the trailhead.
3.9 (**Option:** Bridge over Yosemite Creek adds about 0.1 mile to hike)
7.6 Arrive back at Upper Yosemite Falls Trailhead

7 Yosemite Falls from Tioga Road

This is a longer but arguably easier way to reach the top of Yosemite Falls than climbing straight up from the valley floor. The mostly forested up-and-down trail follows Yosemite Creek, hopping or wading several of its tributaries to where the stream, compressed between narrow walls, gathers speed and force and shoots out over the north rim in a series of steps totaling 2,425 feet into the valley. You can stand very close to the edge where the falls begin, and, if the water is high, get soaked and half-stunned by the spray and the roar. There is camping nearby.

Height of falls: 2,425 feet
Start: Yosemite Creek Trailhead on Tioga Road or Yosemite Creek Campground
Distance: 16.0 miles out and back from Tioga Road (12.4 if you start from Yosemite Creek Campground)
Hiking time: 8–14 hours
Elevation change: 1,000 feet
Difficulty: Moderate as a backpack, strenuous as a day hike
Seasons: Best after early June when the snow is gone and before mid-Aug when the creek and the falls are dry
Nearest facilities: Food, water, toilets, and gas at Crane Flat
Permits: None for a day hike; required for overnights in advance, or first-come, first-served from the wilderness centers in Yosemite Valley or Tuolumne Meadows

Maps: USGS Yosemite Falls quad
Special considerations: If the Yosemite Creek Campground is open, you can shorten this hike round-trip to 12.4 miles and about 600 feet elevation change. The obscurely marked road to the campground is about 0.2 mile east of the White Wolf turnoff from Tioga Road and easy to miss. The marked White Wolf turnoff is on the left (north) side of the road. The campground road is on the right. Drive several miles down a steep, narrow, sometimes one-lane winding road to the campground. There are restrooms there but no campground host and not much else, though the campground is maintained. At the very beginning of the campground is a sturdy bridge over Yosemite Creek. Just on the other side of the bridge on the right, you will see a sign marked "Yosemite Falls 6.2 miles."

Finding the trailhead: On Tioga Road (CA 120), drive about 20 miles east of Crane Flat or 26 miles west of Tuolumne Meadows. There is parking on both sides of the highway. The Ten Lakes Trail departs from the north side, the Yosemite Creek Trail from the south. The trail begins at the west end of the parking area. Trailhead GPS: N37 51.07' / W119 34.40'

The Hike

From the trailhead sign descend through lodgepole pines to cross Yosemite Creek, which can be difficult in early season when the water is high, then descend more gradually until you reach the Yosemite Creek Campground at 1.5 miles. Follow the paved road all the way through the campground and over a bridge. Just after crossing another, smaller branch of the creek, turn left at a sign marked "Trail Junction" and leave the road and the campground at 2.2 miles.

The trail wanders through fairly flat forest, then climbs over a rocky shoulder marked with ducks where the route is obscure. Some handsome junipers grow from cracks in the rock. Shortly after dropping from this shoulder, a trail cuts back to the right (northwest) at 3.7 miles, heading toward Lukens Lake and White Wolf. Continue straight ahead (south) and cross a tributary of Yosemite Creek. There are a few campsites here.

Gradually the smooth rounded granite walls force the trail and the creek into a narrow defile, and the lovely aquamarine water races over the smooth rock in hypnotic swirling patterns. Then the valley widens and the creek and trail meander more slowly through the forest, where more good campsites can be found. Cross Blue Jay Creek carefully on

Yosemite Creek gathers itself to make the leap into Yosemite Valley.

rocks that are sometimes slippery, then cross two wide, sandy flats, reenter the forest, and meet the Eagle Peak Trail in a ferny glen at 7.3 miles. Continue straight ahead (south) and cross another tributary of Yosemite Creek. There are a few campsites here.

Turn left at this junction for a few yards, then follow signs to the overlook through sculpted rocks and twisted Jeffrey pines to an iron railing. Directly across the valley the upside-down bowl of Sentinel Dome rises alone to the west of Glacier Point. Farther in the distance is Mount Starr King, also somewhat rounded and isolated from the surrounding ridges. Half Dome is on the left and the Clark Range is on the horizon. The path now drops down a series of steep and slippery steps cut into the cliff to a platform protected by more iron railings. The roar, the drenching spray, and the dizzying drop over the falls is exhilarating, but not for the faint of heart or the acrophobic. For a different perspective return to the main trail and turn right (southeast), continuing on for 0.1 mile to a footbridge that spans Yosemite Creek a few yards upstream from the brink.

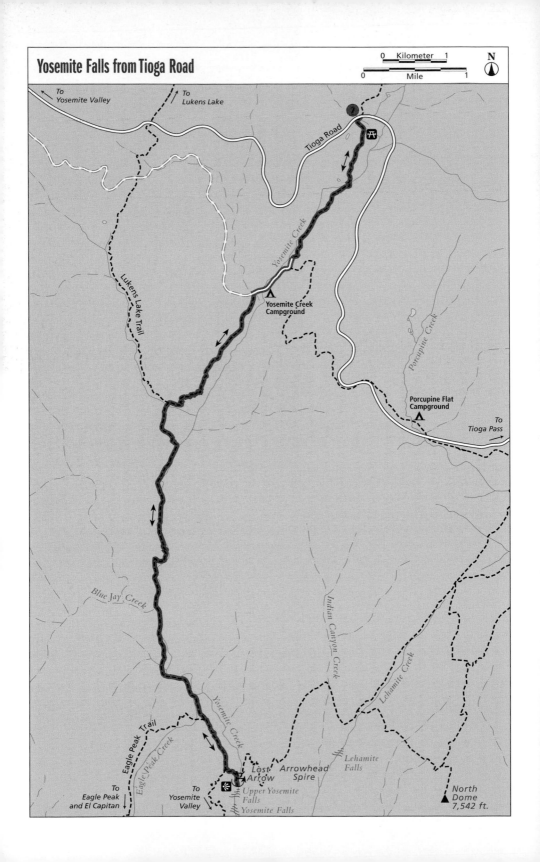

Yosemite Falls from Tioga Road

0   Kilometer   1

0   Mile   1

N

To Yosemite Valley

To Lukens Lake

Tioga Road

7

Yosemite Creek

Lukens Lake Trail

Yosemite Creek Campground

Porcupine Creek

Porcupine Flat Campground

To Tioga Pass

Blue Jay Creek

Indian Canyon Creek

Lehamite Creek

Eagle Peak Trail

Eagle Peak Creek

Yosemite Creek

Lost Arrow

Arrowhead Spire

Lehamite Falls

To Eagle Peak and El Capitan

To Yosemite Valley

Upper Yosemite Falls

Yosemite Falls

North Dome 7,542 ft.

Most of Yosemite Valley is revealed from the top of Yosemite Falls.

You can return the way you came, or if you are planning to spend the night, retrace your steps to the main trail and follow it back upstream along the west side of the creek before pitching your tent. The area just at the top of the falls is trampled and overused, and camping within 0.25 mile of the rim is prohibited anyway.

Miles and Directions

0.0 Yosemite Creek Trailhead

1.5 Yosemite Creek Campground; follow the paved road through the middle

2.2 End of campground; leave the road and turn left

3.7 Lukens Lake Trail junction; continue straight ahead

7.5 Eagle Peak Trail junction; continue straight ahead

8.0 Yosemite Falls; turn left to the overlook

16.0 Arrive back at the Yosemite Creek Trailhead

Option: If you can arrange a shuttle to take you back to your starting point on Tioga Road, you can continue your hike from the top of the falls on down into Yosemite Valley 3.8 miles below.

8 Bridalveil Fall

Bridalveil Creek pours over the southern wall of Yosemite Valley through a defile between Cathedral Rocks and the Leaning Tower. But before it reaches the bottom 620 feet below, the wind catches, tatters, and flings the droplets into graceful, lacy patterns. Bridalveil seldom lets you down. It's one of the few waterfalls in Yosemite that flows year-round. Its source, Bridalveil Creek, runs through a relatively broad valley with deep soil and plenty of vegetation that collects and stores water from winter snows, which it releases slowly throughout the year. Yosemite Falls and many others that flow into the valley are often dry by midsummer.

Height of fall: 620 feet
Start: Bridalveil Fall Trailhead
Distance: 0.4 mile out and back
Hiking time: One-half to 1 hour
Elevation change: 50 feet
Difficulty: Easy
Seasons: Spring, summer, and fall. Icy and dangerous in winter.

Nearest facilities: Toilets but no water at the trailhead
Permits: None
Maps: USGS El Capitan quad, but a map isn't necessary
Special considerations: Stay off the sharp and slippery rocks at the base of the fall. Serious injuries have occurred here.

Finding the trailhead: The parking lot for the fall is located on the Wawona Road (CA 41) about 1.5 miles after you emerge from the east portal of the Wawona Tunnel and before the road splits into Northside and Southside Drives, which are one-way roads. Watch carefully for the sign on the right (southeast). If you miss it, you'll have to drive partway around the valley to get back. You cannot approach the waterfall by road directly from the east. The parking lot is very busy. Be prepared to wait a few minutes for a space midday. Unfortunately, the Yosemite Valley shuttle bus doesn't come this far, but you can take the El Capitan shuttle that runs only in summer, get off at stop E6, Cathedral Beach, and walk to the trailhead. Trailhead GPS: N37 48.00' / W119 39.04'

The Hike

Follow the signs up a wide paved path to a fork at 0.1 mile. Climb the right (south) fork along the tumbling boulder-strewn stream to the vista point near the base of the fall at 0.2 mile. In spring, when the fall is in full spate, you are bound to get soaked from the spray. The flow diminishes in summer and by autumn is sometimes reduced to a filmy mist. But when the flow from melting snow is at its height, the force of the water crashing into the rocks at the base is thrown so high it looks as though the fall is flowing uphill. On sunny afternoons rainbows are almost guaranteed.

This fall is beautiful in winter too but is best admired from a distance then since the approach to the base can be icy.

Bridalveil Fall sometimes flows so powerfully that it is flung back uphill from the base.

A rainbow forms over Bridalveil Fall on sunny afternoons.

The view of Bridalveil from Northside Drive is a favorite.

Miles and Directions

0.0 Parking lot trailhead
0.1 Trail fork turns right
0.2 Vista point
0.4 Arrive back at the trailhead

Option A: Another way to enjoy Bridalveil Fall away from the usual crowds is to take a hike along the old Big Oak Flat Road (no longer open to traffic), which you pick up from Northside Drive just across the street from the curve in the Merced River known as the Devil's Elbow. Follow the abandoned road westward for about a mile for an elevated and very grand view of the fall across the valley.

Option B: You can't reach the knickpoint (the very spot at the top where the creek drops over the cliff edge), but you can get views of the fall from several viewpoints along the south rim's Pohono Trail. You can also visit the source of the fall, Bridalveil Creek, by hiking from McGurk Meadow off the Glacier Point Road to pick up the Pohono Trail and follow it to the right (east) for about a half mile to pretty Bridalveil Creek, an out-and-back hike of 3.9 miles.

9 Silver Strand Fall

This is a lovely waterfall, but very few visitors to Yosemite ever see it even though it is 580 feet high. That's because it flows over the cliff just above and behind the Tunnel View parking lot, the spot where everybody is turned in the opposite direction photographing one another against the glorious backdrop of Yosemite Valley. Silver Strand is an ephemeral fall and is usually dry by mid-July, but if you are there early enough in the season, there is great satisfaction in pointing it out to visitors who come to Yosemite often but have never known it was there. It is tucked back into a shallow alcove but is visible all day—it's best viewed in mid- to late afternoon. This one is especially pretty in winter too.

There is no trail to the base of the fall, nor can you hike to the top since the creek that is its source makes a steep, dangerous drop before it plunges over the cliff. You can, however, take a hike along the Pohono Trail to the fall's source, the stream known as Meadow Brook, burbling down the slope through a garden of wildflowers and flowing right across the trail.

Height of fall: 580 feet
Start: Tunnel View parking lot
Distance: Not applicable
Hiking time: Minutes
Elevation change: Not applicable
Difficulty: Not applicable
Seasons: Spring, early summer, occasionally in winter
Nearest facilities: Yosemite Village, Curry (Half Dome) Village. No gas in Yosemite Valley.
Permits: None

Maps: Any Yosemite road map (El Capitan USGS topo if you plan to hike to Meadow Brook)
Finding the viewpoint/trailhead: Drive CA 41, Wawona Road, through the tunnel to its east end (watch out for pedestrians) and park in one of the two lots on each side of the road. There is a sign for the Pohono Trailhead in the rear of the upper parking lot. Trailhead GPS: N37 42.56' / W119 40.37'

Miles and Directions to Meadow Brook

0.0 Pohono Trailhead from south parking lot

0.2 Turn right at a short unmarked cutoff trail and walk a few steps to the viewpoint that was formerly Inspiration Point.

1.0 Continue straight ahead at a junction heading to Artist Point and Bridalveil Fall.

1.9 Continue to follow the Pohono Trail to Meadow Brook.

3.8 Arrive back at the trailhead.

Option: Hike to Meadow Brook, source of Silver Strand Fall. You will find the signed trailhead at the back of the upper of two Tunnel View parking lots. This is the start of

Silver Strand begins to flow on warm winter days. ▶

Silver Strand is a major waterfall often missed by visitors.

the Pohono Trail that goes along the south rim of the valley all the way to Glacier Point. Meadow Brook is 3.8 miles along this trail. You must be truly motivated see Meadow Brook since this hike involves a steady climb of 2,600 feet. After the first half hour, you might decide to descend and enjoy Silver Strand from the parking lot after all.

You do get to experience a bit of Yosemite history if you continue the climb. Along the way you pass a short spur trail to the original Inspiration Point (shown on the topo as "Old Inspiration Point"). Then a bit later you pass another spot marked on the topo as "Inspiration Point." This is where the Wawona Stage and Auto Road into the valley was located before the Wawona Tunnel was built in the 1930s.

10 Ribbon Fall

There is no trail to the base of Ribbon Fall and no access to the point where it dives off the northern rim of Yosemite Valley, but it is one of the most spectacular of the valley's waterfalls, and there are several places where you can get a good view. It's 1,612 feet high, the highest free-falling plunge in Yosemite, the highest single drop in North America, and one of the very highest in the world.

Height of fall: 1,612 feet
Start: Northside or Southside Drive, wherever you like the view
Distance: Varies
Hiking time: As long as you like
Elevation change: None
Difficulty: Easy

Seasons: Apr, May, early June
Nearest facilities: Yosemite Village or Half Dome (Curry) Village
Permits: None, unless you plan to backpack to Ribbon Meadow. Available in the wilderness center in Yosemite Valley.
Maps: El Capitan

Finding the trailhead: There is no trail to the fall itself, but you can get a good view from Southside Drive near Bridalveil Fall. Since the 2017 Ferguson Fire, you can see the fall through the downed trees from Southside Drive toward the west end of the valley, but if you're driving, have your passenger look for it.

The Hike

By the time Ribbon Fall reaches the bottom (at least as far as you can see to the bottom), it's no more than a dense mist, though early in the season its stream reaches and occasionally floods Northside Drive. It drains a fairly small area of forest and meadow, which is surrounded by glacially scoured rock that does not retain water very long after the winter snow melts. In a wet year it may run into July but is usually at its finest earlier in the spring. It's easy to miss from the valley floor when your eye is caught by nearby torrents like Yosemite Falls, but once you have spotted it, you'll be smugly pointing it out to others who might never have noticed it before. For the best view, look across the valley from Bridalveil Fall, from the Pohono Trail on the south rim, or from Valley View on the north side.

▶ According to one ethnographer, the Indian name of this fall meant "graceful." A European lady is said to have called it "Virgin's Tears" because it doesn't last very long. Joseph Bunnell, a student of the Miwok language, called it Pigeon Creek Fall. He said Indians called it "Pigeon Basket," meaning Pigeon Nest. A later Yosemite promoter, Hutchings, named it "Ribbon Fall" because "an English name is desirable."

Ribbon Fall pours over the north rim early in the season.

Ribbon Creek flows only in springtime.

Miles and Directions to Ribbon Creek

0.0   Tamarack Flat Campground

2.0   Junction with path marked "Foresta"; keep left

2.1   Cross bridge over Cascade Creek

3.8   Old Big Oak Flat Road; turn right

4.4   Turn left off the road onto trail

7.4   Ribbon Meadow and Ribbon Creek

14.8   Arrive back at the trailhead

Option: If you are intrigued enough to explore the source of Ribbon Fall, though you can't get to the very tipping point, you can make a fine day hike from Tamarack Flat Campground, or better yet, a short backpack along the Old Big Oak Flat Road trail to the El Capitan Trail and Ribbon Creek.

Finding the Trailhead to Tamarack Campground: Drive the Tioga Road 3 miles east of Crane Flat to the signed Tamarack Flat Campground on the south side of the road, 3 miles down. After a short walk along an old road, followed by an invigorating climb, the path meanders along soggy Ribbon Meadow to Ribbon Creek, where there is a nice campsite. Don't try to continue along the creek to the top of the fall, as the slope is much too steep and dangerous. Though as long as you have come this far, you can continue along the trail to El Capitan. The distance is roughly 15 miles round-trip with about 1,700 feet of elevation change.

11 Cascade Creek Falls

You will pass this big, spectacular series of falls and cascades as you enter Yosemite Valley by any of the park's entrances. Here, Cascade Creek and Tamarack Creek tumble down from the north to a point just below the Big Oak Flat Road, where they join to form a formidable 500-foot torrent known as the Cascades before dropping the rest of the way down to meet the Merced River. Unlike many of Yosemite Valley's falls, they flow for most of the year. This short hike on a rather obscure trail will take you to what is probably the only free-falling section of the Cascades. You'll be close enough to get wet.

Some drivers entering the valley miss the Cascades altogether. Most of the viewpoints from roads are frustratingly either too close or too far away for satisfying photos, but two of them are worthwhile. One of the best is a mile or so west of the Wawona Tunnel on CA 41. Another is from a turnout on the right off Big Oak Flat Road just east of the last of a series of short tunnels. Here you must exit the last tunnel slowly to join a tangle of cars trying squeeze into or out of a turnout too small to accommodate all of them. The best place to see this waterfall by far is from the bridge over Cascade Creek on CA 140, just east of the park entrance kiosk. You will be too close to see the falls top to bottom, but you will be face-to-face with the prettiest section, where the water is in free fall.

Height of fall: 100 feet
Start: Parking area on bridge over Cascade Creek
Distance: 0.5 mile out and back
Hiking time: 40 minutes
Elevation change: 100 feet

Difficulty: Moderate
Seasons: Spring, summer, fall; icy and dangerous in winter
Nearest facilities: El Portal. None at trailhead.
Permits: None
Maps: El Capitan

Finding the trailhead: From the Arch Rock Entrance to Yosemite, drive CA 140 about 2.7 miles to the bridge over Cascade Creek. There is parking on both sides of the road. The "official" viewpoint complete with interpretive signs is on the left (north) side. From Yosemite Valley, driving west on Northside Drive, keep right at the point where the left lane curves back over the Merced to return to the valley. Continue straight ahead on CA 140, passing the turnoff to CA 120 (Big Oak Flat Road) and Tuolumne Meadows on the right. Parking for Cascade Falls view is 1.7 miles ahead. Trailhead GPS: N37 43.26' / W119 42.16'

The Hike

From the turnout on the bridge over Cascade Creek, you can get a partial view of the waterfall nicely framed by trees, but you will definitely want more. For a

The base of Cascade Falls can be reached by a short trail.

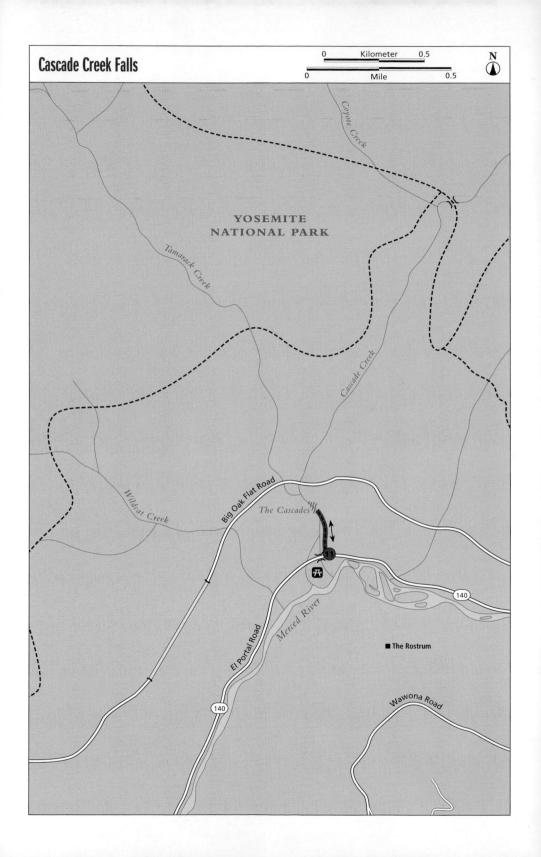

Cascade Creek Falls

YOSEMITE
NATIONAL PARK

Coyote Creek

Tamarack Creek

Cascade Creek

Wildcat Creek

Big Oak Flat Road

The Cascades

El Portal Road

Merced River

140

The Rostrum

Wawona Road

140

N

0   Kilometer   0.5

0   Mile   0.5

Sections of Cascade Falls can be seen from Big Oak Flat Road and CA 140.

close-up look, walk carefully along the narrow verge on the north side of the road eastward for about 40 yards, keeping an eye out for oncoming traffic on your right while watching for a faint path heading off uphill to the left. There is no sign. Climb upward along the winding path over uneven ground, avoiding fallen branches and holes as well as occasional pipes, wires, and other small man-made structures left from the days when the precursor to the highway made a stop here. After you have gained some altitude, the path makes a gradual curve toward the left and the roar of the falls becomes louder and louder, the mist more and more dense. A low concrete barrier is the best spot for a photo. Do not be tempted to scramble out onto the boulders in the streambed to get closer to the falls. This is a free-falling torrent, unbelievably powerful and deadly at high water, and the jumbled rocks are sharp, slippery, and dangerous at any time of year.

Miles and Directions

0.0 Cascade Creek bridge parking area on CA 140

0.25 Barrier facing Cascade Falls

0.5 Arrive back at the trailhead

12 Upper Cascade Creek Cascades

You will pass this big, spectacular series of falls and cascades as you enter Yosemite Valley by any of the park's entrances, though they are easy to miss from the roads. Cascade Creek and Tamarack Creek tumble down from the north to a point just below the Big Oak Flat Road, where they join to form a formidable 500-foot torrent known as the Cascades before dropping the rest of the way down to meet the Merced River.

The section of Cascade Creek that forms a true waterfall is only visible a few steps from a parking turnout on CA 140. If you're intrigued by where this beautiful fall comes from and want to see more, there's an easy trail to one of Cascade Creek's prettiest upper sections. It begins from Tamarack Flat Campground off Tioga Road down to a bridge where the creek roars and rumbles in spring and early summer, then subsides to form interesting swimming holes and flower gardens later on. It flows all year but may be no more than a trickle by late August.

Height of fall: Indeterminate
Start: Tamarack Flat Campground beyond site #5
Distance: 4.2 miles out and back
Hiking time: 2 hours as a day hike, overnight as a backpack
Elevation change: 500 feet
Difficulty: Easy
Seasons: Whenever Tioga Road is open, best in spring and early summer

Nearest facilities: Water and toilets at Tamarack Flat Campground
Permits: None for a day hike. Available in advance or first-come, first-served from the wilderness centers in Tuolumne Meadows or Yosemite Valley.
Maps: USGS Tamarack Flat and El Capitan quads

Finding the trailhead: Drive the Tioga Road (CA 120) 3 miles east of Crane Flat to the signed Tamarack Flat Campground turnoff on the south side of the road. A series of tight, sometimes blind, hairpin turns descends 3 miles to the campground. Park in the obvious parking area near the entrance, and walk the short distance to the trailhead just past campsite #5. There are bear boxes at the trailhead, but not at the parking area. Trailhead GPS: N37 45.06' / W119 44.12'

The Hike

Follow the abandoned, partly paved road that continues on past the campground through an area that was badly burned during the 2013 Rim Fire but is alive with fire-following bracken ferns and wildflowers crowding into the newly created openings. Poking up from the greenery on the forest floor is an odd collection of enormous granite boulders that resemble a kind of disordered and partially melted

A bridge crosses over a scenic section of Cascade Creek.

Upper Cascade Creek Cascades

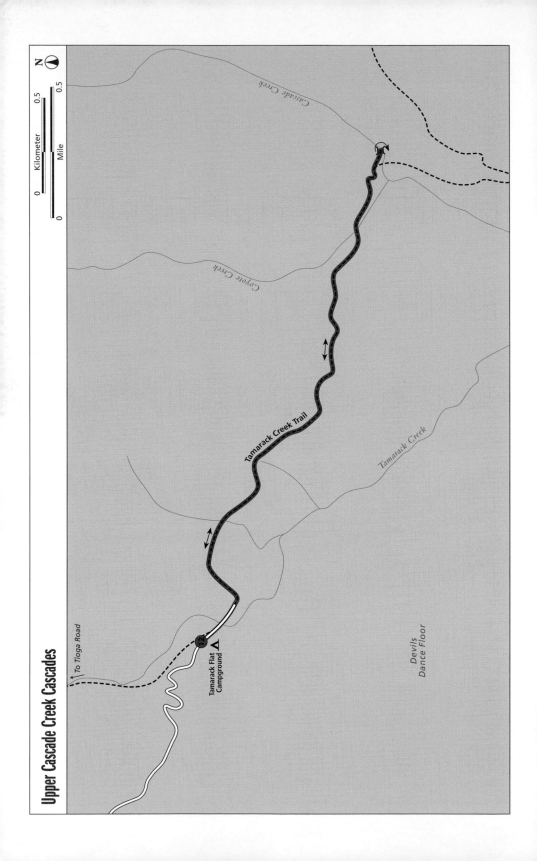

Good swimming holes can be found on upper Cascade Creek.

Stonehenge. Beyond these, the road continues gently downhill, now and then interrupted by rocky washouts and flowery little streams. Alongside, little meadows alternate with crowded stands of baby trees elbowing one another for space to grow big enough to rebuild the forest. The grade slowly becomes steeper and the sound of running water gets noisier.

At mile 2 reach a junction where your trail makes a sharp turn to the left. Ignore an inconspicuous sign pointing straight ahead marked "Foresta," where an unmaintained and overgrown path leads southwest. Your planned route follows the sign that says "El Capitan 6 miles." Your goal is just beyond this sign where a sturdy bridge crosses Cascade Creek. It is not as free-falling here as it appears downstream, but it foams and crashes over the rocks steeply enough to satisfy anybody's waterfall craving. The setting is exquisite, especially in early season, with arrangements of fragrant white azaleas and clumps of big, round-leaved Indian rhubarb in the quieter pools, and creek dogwood lining the banks. A popular campsite occupies a rise to the right of the trail just past the bridge. Since this spot lies along the most convenient route to the top of El Capitan and other destinations along the north rim of Yosemite Valley, you'll meet plenty of other hikers pausing here to rest and refill water bottles.

Western azaleas bloom alongside Cascade Creek in spring.

Miles and Directions

0.0 Tamarack Flat Campground trailhead

2.0 Junction with unmaintained path marked "Foresta"; turn left

2.1 Bridge over Cascade Creek

4.2 Arrive back at the trailhead

Option: If you have time, and especially if you have kids: Enjoy the main cascade, then return to the inconspicuous Foresta sign and follow that overgrown trail for no more than 0.2 mile to a quiet pond where a tributary of Cascade Creek crosses the path. A miniature waterfall trickles into the pool in a ferny and flowery setting complete with a little rock cave. This is the sweetest, most inviting, perfectly proportioned loafing or wading spot you've ever seen, and you will want to take a dip or at least dangle your toes as long as you can stand the chilly water.

13 Sentinel Fall

Sentinel Fall is the second-highest waterfall in Yosemite Valley at 2,000 feet, though its graceful, slender profile and almost straight downward course makes it appear even taller. It's visible from many spots in the center and the north side of the valley floor (as long as you're at least a half mile west of Camp 4), and also from the north rim. It is immediately west of the big flat vertical slab of Sentinel Rock and is best seen around noon. Like Bridalveil, it pours off the south rim as a hanging valley waterfall, a former stream that dropped over the rim after the main valley was excavated by glaciers on a course perpendicular to the stream. It can't quite be called ephemeral since it often lasts well into summer, but it does not flow year-round. You can't reach the base from the valley floor, but you can hike to the top. The creek flows through such a narrow defile that you can't see it all the way down, but the short sections you can see are thrilling. The hike along the Pohono Trail to get to Sentinel Creek takes you past several spectacular south rim viewpoints into and across Yosemite Valley including El Capitan, Ribbon, and Yosemite Falls.

Height of fall: 2,000 feet
Start: Taft Point / Sentinel Dome Trailhead
Distance: 4.4 miles out and back
Hiking time: 3 hours
Elevation change: About 700 feet
Difficulty: Easy
Seasons: Spring and early summer, though the Pohono Trail is open through fall. Glacier Point Road is closed past Badger Flat in winter.
Nearest facilities: Pit toilet at trailhead, food, water, toilets, phone at Glacier Point
Permits: None for a day hike. Available in advance or from the wilderness center in Yosemite Valley for overnights.
Maps: USGS Half Dome quad

Special considerations: The Glacier Point Road ends at Glacier Point itself, where there is a big parking lot, but by midmorning it's usually full. If you get a late start, you will probably have to drive to Chinquapin junction on Wawona Road, where you will be directed to the Badger Pass ski area to wait until there is space available. There are plans to provide a shuttle bus to Glacier Point, but ask about it at the visitor center first. You start at the Taft Point / Sentinel Dome Trailheads on the left whether or not the shuttle is operating. If you have reservations at the Bridalveil Creek Campground or have a wilderness permit for an overnight trip leaving from the Glacier Point Road, you can drive through.

Finding the trailhead: If you start early enough, before 9 a.m. from Yosemite Valley, for example (see "Special Considerations," above), drive about 14 miles west on the Wawona Road (CA 41) to Chinquapin junction. Turn left (east) and follow the Glacier Point Road for 13 miles to the signed Taft Point / Sentinel Dome Trailhead on the left. Trailhead GPS: N37 43.39' / W119 34.27'

Sentinel Fall flows down to the valley beside Sentinel Rock.

The Hike

From the trailhead just a few feet downhill from the parking lot and toilet, turn left at the junction marked "Taft Point" and "Sentinel Dome." Contour along the dry slope and pass an interesting and mysterious geological feature, a big pile of pure white quartz beside the trail. Continue on downhill past lupine and minty-smelling pennyroyal for 0.5 mile to meet a junction with the Pohono Trail marked "Sentinel Dome." Turn right (east) here and descend moderately, catching glimpses of the dome ahead through the trees. In another 0.5 mile the trail comes close to the rim, where you can make short detours for spectacular views of El Capitan (the top of which is seldom seen from the valley) and Yosemite Falls. As you hike, you'll pick up the roar of Sentinel Fall

Sentinel Fall is one of Yosemite Valley's tallest waterfalls.

long before you will be able to see it. You'll be tempted to try to slither down toward the rim, but the way is unstable and dangerous.

Cross to the eastern side of unmarked Sentinel Creek, using logs if the water is high. The creek is lined with shrubs blooming with bunches of Labrador tea. On the east side of the creek are some flat granite slabs from which you can catch glimpses of the upper part of the falls. Lower down, the falls are tucked too far back behind the cliff to be visible all the way to the bottom.

▶ **The view of the valley is spectacular here; sometimes you can see all the way westward to the smog of the Central Valley. Notice how, across the valley, Yosemite Falls seems to flow perversely through a cramped narrow notch on the right, while it bypasses the obvious deeper and wider gully to the left. Thousands of years ago, Yosemite Creek did flow down this westernmost route, but a glacier grinding its way down this canyon blocked the creek's usual route permanently so that the water had to find a new way over the cliff.**

Sentinel Fall can only be seen in glimpses from the top.

When you have had enough, return the way you came, or continue eastward along the Pohono Trail, pausing at Stanford, Crocker, and Dewey Point overlooks all the way to Glacier Point.

Miles and Directions

0.0 Taft Point / Sentinel Dome Trailhead

0.5 Junction with the Pohono Trail

2.2 Sentinel Creek

4.4 Arrive back at the trailhead

14 Illilouette Fall

Illilouette Fall flows from Illilouette Creek, the largest tributary of the Merced River. It is a big, spectacular fall, but it's tucked up into a notch in a side canyon where most people don't notice it. There is a distant view from the beginning of the John Muir Trail, just a short distance toward the Vernal Fall Bridge, but most people don't know to look for it. This hike along the Panorama Trail from Glacier Point will take you to the very top of the fall, where you can get close enough to feel the spray.

It flows straight down from the top through a narrow gorge for part of the way, but then bumps down in a very long cascade to reach the Merced River, where the rock below is much more jointed than the more massive granite on either side of the gorge and has been fractured by ice. It is easiest to see midday, and while you seldom get a glance of the entire vertical drop from the bottom, the huge cloud of mist it produces early in the season is impressive.

Height of fall: 370 feet
Start: Panorama / Pohono Trailhead at Glacier Point
Distance: 4.2 miles out and back
Hiking time: 3–4 hours
Elevation change: 1,500 feet
Difficulty: Moderate
Seasons: All summer, whenever Glacier Point Road is open
Nearest facilities: Food, phones, water, toilets at Glacier Point
Permits: None

Maps: USGS Half Dome quad
Special considerations: The Glacier Point Road ends at Glacier Point itself, where there is a big parking lot, but by midmorning it's usually full. If you get a late start, you will probably have to drive to the Chinquapin junction on Wawona Road, where you will be directed to the Badger Pass ski area to wait until there is space available at Glacier Point. There are plans to provide a shuttle bus to Glacier Point, but ask about it at the visitor center first.

Finding the trailhead: If you start the drive to Glacier Point early enough (9–10 a.m.), you can drive from Yosemite Valley to Chinquapin on CA 41, then turn left and drive 16 miles all the way to Glacier Point at the end of the road. Trailhead GPS: N37 43.67' / W119 34.40'

The Hike

From the parking lot, hike directly toward Half Dome to a spot overlooking an outdoor amphitheater. You will want to take a minute to recover from the overwhelming immensity of the panorama from Glacier Point before setting off. To the left is North Dome, capping the graceful Royal Arches; in the center is Half Dome, the monumental symbol of Yosemite. Tenaya Canyon stretches away to the northeast, and to the west runs the Merced River Canyon, down whose Giant Staircase flow Vernal and Nevada Falls. Now, walk a few steps uphill to the right to locate the trailhead sign.

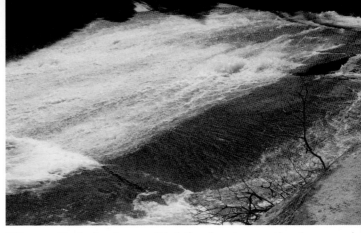

Illilouette Creek slips down a slide before dropping over the edge.

From the sign turn right (east) to find the Panorama and Pohono Trail junction at 0.1 mile. The Panorama Trail heads left (south) toward Illilouette Fall. The first mile of trail switchbacks downward through an area burned several years ago. Fragrant ceanothus and chinquapin with its spiny green fruits line the path. This is a good place to listen for the booming call of the sooty grouse in spring and early summer. At 1.2 miles a trail coming from Mono Meadow joins this one from the south. Keep left (northeast) and continue to descend into Illilouette Gorge. Shrubs give way to forest and the rush of Illilouette Creek becomes audible. Watch for a little path to the left of the trail where you can get your best view of the fall. There used to be a protective railing, but it is no longer there, and the rock at the edge of the cliff is very slippery—don't get too close. Just before the trail reaches the footbridge over the fall, you might spot what appear to be several idyllic campsites on the right, but camping is not permitted here. It's too near the water, too near the trail, and too near the road. It's a nice spot for a rest and a snack though. The entire fall is not visible from the footbridge, but the creek cascades down in picturesque wedding-cake fashion near the top, and in springtime the blooms of western azaleas lining the banks perfume the air. Enjoy the fall, then return the way you came.

▶ **Nobody knows what *Illilouette* means. It has been assumed to be either corrupted French or a Native American word. Despite much study and speculation, the mystery has never been solved.**

Miles and Directions

0.0   Glacier Point

0.1   Panorama / Pohono Trail junction; turn left

1.2   Mono Meadow Trail junction; keep left

2.1   Illilouette Fall bridge

4.2   Arrive back at Glacier Point

◀   *The spray from Illilouette in springtime lights up the canyon.*

15 Staircase Fall

Staircase Fall does not gush or roar, its flow is not especially copious, and it seldom flows past early July, but many Yosemite waterfall lovers consider this to be the most beautiful fall in Yosemite Valley. It is surely the most unusual. It descends for 1,300 feet (though you can't see the top) from a shady bowl near Glacier Point, then follows an angular path of regularly spaced stairsteps that descend eastward, one by one, to end above the Curry (Half Dome) Village parking lot. It's a great favorite of those who know where to find it. It is possible to miss this fall altogether if you are not looking for it, even though it flows over a nearby open expanse of rock, since there is a chance you will be hunting for a parking space or focused on finding pizza or ice cream. It is easiest to appreciate in the afternoon or when the sky is overcast, and is especially striking after a fresh snowfall when the frosted ledges remind you of a beautiful, if lopsided, wedding cake.

Height of fall: 1,300 feet
Start: Half Dome (Curry) Village parking lot
Distance: A few steps, or as long a section of the Valley Loop Trail as you like
Hiking time: As long as you like
Elevation change: None

Difficulty: Easy
Seasons: April to June or after a hard rain
Nearest facilities: Half Dome (Curry) Village
Permits: None
Maps: USGS Half Dome quad

Finding the trailhead: You don't need to hike to this one, though it makes a nice stop on a hike along the Valley Loop Trail, which runs around the periphery of Yosemite Valley. You can also ride the free shuttle bus from anywhere in the valley and get off at stop 14 or 20.

The Hike

You can hike from anyplace along the Valley Loop Trail to a spot above and just east of Half Dome (Curry) Village. On the other hand, you can just pull into the Half Dome (Curry) Village parking lot and look up to get the very best view of this unusual waterfall.

Staircase Fall is the only one of its kind in Yosemite. ▶

16 Lehamite Fall

You can't get very close to Lehamite Fall, but it's big and is a major tributary of the Merced River, at 1,180 feet high. It continues to flow after many of the valley's other north-side falls are dry. During spring snowmelt when Yosemite Valley's north rim becomes a veritable gallery of waterfalls, Lehamite Creek, just east of Yosemite Falls, plunges down a deep gorge, meets Indian Canyon, jumps a barrier, and becomes a long, long, silvery white stream that contrasts sharply with the dark rocks and conifer forest behind it. Since the narrow notch that contains it faces west, it's invisible east of Yosemite Village, but there are clear and dramatic views from the valley floor from Cook's Meadow, from near the chapel, and from several spots right in the center of Yosemite Village, especially in the afternoon. You just have to remember to look up.

It is one of the few waterfalls that retains its original Native American name, which means "arrow wood" according to one scholar. The gorge itself through which Lehamite Creek runs is still called Indian Canyon because it was used by the local people as a route out of the valley into the high country.

Height of fall: 1,180 feet
Start: Cook's Meadow
Distance: Negligible
Hiking time: Minutes or as long as you like
Elevation change: None
Difficulty: Easy

Seasons: April, May, June
Nearest facilities: Yosemite Village
Permits: None
Maps: Half Dome, Yosemite Falls, but none needed

Finding the trailhead: Ride the valley shuttle to stop 6, 7, or 11 and wander out into the meadow until the fall comes into view.

The Hike

Follow the boardwalk out into Cook's Meadow, Sentinel Meadow, or Sentinel Bridge. If you stand in the right place, you can get a great photo of both Lehamite and Yosemite Falls in the same shot, and you'll be surprised that you hadn't noticed it before. If you feel a need for greater intimacy with Lehamite Fall, you can make an all-day hike to its source from the Porcupine Creek Trailhead off the Tioga Road, heading south toward North Dome, then pick up the trail that skirts Lehamite Creek to within a mile of the falls.

Two of Yosemite's tallest falls can be seen from Cook's Meadow in spring.

17 Upper Snow Creek Falls

Snow Creek drops 2,000 feet in a series of falls, cascades, and even a waterwheel or two all the way from May Lake to Tenaya Creek, not far above the Mirror Lake loop trail. Unfortunately, you can't see most of it, even when it is running high in spring, except by telescope or powerful telephoto lens from Half Dome. A portion is said to be visible from the bottom by climbing up from the upper end of the Mirror Lake loop, but there is no trail and the climb from the base is dangerous and strongly discouraged by the park service.

You can climb the Snow Creek Trail from the base, also off the Mirror Lake loop, but you don't see the fall for a very long time and it's a grueling climb, though it does allow you a great head-on view of the face of Half Dome you can't get anywhere else. (You can get this same view of Half Dome starting at the top as described below.)

There is a very rewarding way to see the upper section of Snow Creek Falls near the confluence of Snow Creek and Porcupine Creek on a moderate day hike of less than 8 miles. Here the stream pours over an interesting pattern of free falls, cascades, and slides.

The pattern of this fall changes from week to week as the snow melts, and you will wish you could come back over and over again. It's an especially interesting challenge for photographers. There are some good campsites near the upper section of the falls, but for the time being, camping is prohibited here (see "Special Considerations," below).

Height of falls: Indeterminate
Start: Porcupine Creek Trailhead
Distance: 8.0 miles out and back
Hiking time: 4–5 hours
Elevation change: 1,100 feet
Difficulty: Moderate
Seasons: Spring and summer, whenever Tioga Road is open
Nearest facilities: Food, water, phone, gas at Crane Flat
Permits: None for a day hike

Maps: Yosemite Falls
Special considerations: Camping has been prohibited here for several years due to the presence of a female black bear who is not at all aggressive toward humans but has learned to grab your bear canister, fling it over a cliff, then climb down a slope inaccessible to humans, hoping the canister has burst like a piñata, to pick out the treats. Check with the park service before requesting a wilderness permit for this area.

Finding the trailhead: On Tioga Road (CA 120), drive 14 miles west of Tuolumne Meadows or 23 miles east of Crane Flat. The signed Porcupine Creek Trailhead and parking area are on the south side of the road. Trailhead GPS: N37 48.24' / W119 32.43'

Each section of Snow Creek is different from the last. ▶

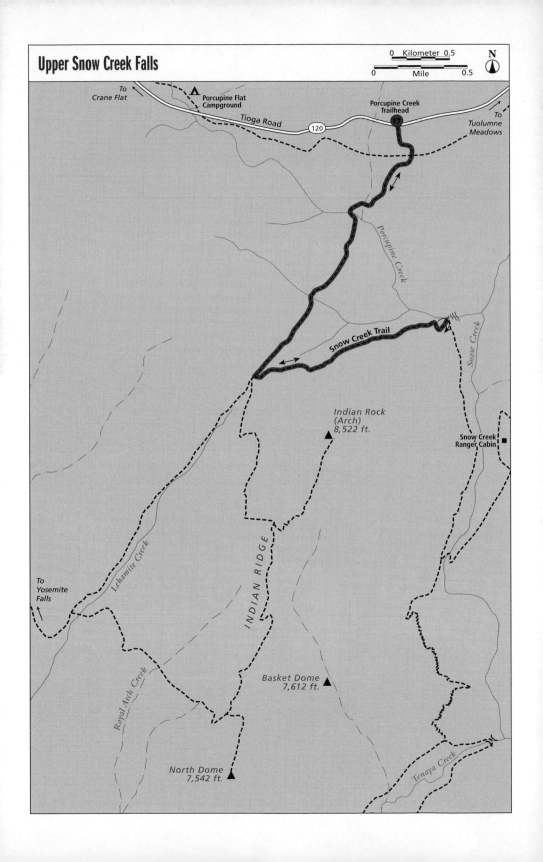

Upper Snow Creek Falls

0 Kilometer 0.5

0 Mile 0.5

N

To Crane Flat

Porcupine Flat Campground

Tioga Road

120

Porcupine Creek Trailhead

17

To Tuolumne Meadows

Porcupine Creek

Snow Creek Trail

Snow Creek

Indian Rock (Arch) 8,522 ft.

Snow Creek Ranger Cabin

Lehamite Creek

INDIAN RIDGE

To Yosemite Falls

Royal Arch Creek

Basket Dome 7,612 ft.

North Dome 7,542 ft.

Tenaya Creek

Water in Snow Creek flows through hidden cracks in the rocks.

The Hike

From the trailhead sign at the east end of the parking area, descend to meet the eroded remains of an old road and follow it downhill until you reach Porcupine Creek at mile 0.7, where what is left of the paving ends. If the water level is high, you can usually find a log crossing upstream. Continue through red fir and lodgepole pine forest, climbing slightly to a trail junction at 2.0 miles. The path straight ahead leads to North Dome, while your route makes a sharp left (northeast) turn and begins an easy descent that becomes steeper as you drop into the Snow Creek drainage. At about 3.5 miles the trail begins another abrupt change of direction as you reach the confluence of Porcupine and Snow Creeks. You'll have to take a few cautious steps off the trail for this springtime wonder of a waterfall to reveal itself, as it does in sections.

The upper part is free-falling, where the water rushes over a narrow overhang so that the space behind the "curtain" is barely visible or is hidden completely. As the summer advances and the volume of water slackens, you can look through the filmy front "curtain" (or absence thereof) into the space behind it, where you may be able to see another curtain of water flowing through a crack in the ceiling above and behind the door . . . a waterfall inside a cave partly hidden by a waterfall at the door of the cave. That's just the beginning. Below, the stream descends a series of broad, flat slabs in swirling patterns, then begins a long slide that vanishes around a curve.

The Snow Creek Trail offers the best view of the face of Half Dome.

You will be tempted to follow the course of the stream to see what happens next by negotiating a steep and unstable slope, but don't do that. Return to the trail above you and follow it down a switchback, where you can see the waterfall from the base all the way to the top.

When you can tear yourself away, head back uphill to the Porcupine Creek Trailhead.

Option: You can make your way back up to Porcupine Creek here, or you can continue to follow Snow Creek southward to a footbridge. You turn left and cross the bridge, where a trail heads back uphill toward Tuolumne Meadows. Or you can pass by the bridge and follow the route straight ahead that drops you via steep, exhausting stairsteps down into Yosemite Valley via Mirror Lake. In either case you will need a car shuttle.

Miles and Directions

- **0.0** Porcupine Creek Trailhead
- **0.7** Cross Porcupine Creek
- **2.0** Junction with the trail to North Dome; turn sharp left (northeast) onto the Snow Creek Trail
- **4.0** Arrive at Snow Creek Falls at the junction of Snow Creek and Porcupine Creek
- **8.0** Return to Porcupine Creek Trailhead

18 Horsetail Fall

This ephemeral waterfall, just east of El Capitan, is easy to miss in the daytime even when it is flowing well, but you will want to pinpoint its location during the day if you plan to see the show it sometimes puts on at sunset in late February. It can be confused with ephemeral Ribbon Fall just west of El Capitan; both can be wispy and may disappear partway down the cliff in a breeze, though Horsetail dries up long before Ribbon does.

Height of fall: 1,325 feet
Start: El Capitan picnic area
Distance: Variable
Hiking time: As long as you like
Elevation change: None
Difficulty: Easy
Seasons: Late winter or spring, or after a hard rain
Nearest facilities: Yosemite Village, Yosemite Lodge
Permits: None
Maps: El Capitan
Special considerations: This waterfall only puts on its spectacular show in late February and only under certain conditions, so everybody is going to try to see it. The viewing is best from the El Capitan picnic area off Northside Drive. If you plan to drive to the nearest spot, you'll need to get there at least two hours before sunset. The "show" happens at dusk, and when it's over hundreds of cars, many driven by people who aren't familiar with the valley, will be trying to find the way back to their lodgings or park exits in the dark, on confusing one-way roads.

Make sure the waterfall is flowing, check the weather report for clear skies, and contact the National Park Service or visitor center for advice or assistance.

Finding the trailhead: From Yosemite Village or Yosemite Lodge, drive one-way Northside Drive westward to the El Capital picnic area. You can't pull into the picnic area to park, but find a spot along the road, on the right side only, as close to the picnic area entrance or exit as possible. Trailhead GPS: GPS: N37 43.38' / W119 37.42'

The Hike

On a night when conditions for seeing the fall are favorable, you could face a very long hike along the road from your car to get to a good viewing spot. You can, of course, take a much longer walk from your campsite or lodging. Depending on where you have found a parking place on Northside Drive, walk along the road to the entrance or exit of the El Capitan picnic area and find a spot where you can get the best view of the fall. Everybody else will be looking in that direction.

At sunset on a clear evening in late February, if conditions are just right, Horsetail Fall (once known as El Capitan Fall) is transformed into a glowing stream of fire. It happens only occasionally when the light of the setting sun strikes the cliff east of El Capitan at precisely the right angle. The sky must be clear and the wind still.

Horsetail Fall is less impressive during the day.

Horsetail Fall seems to glow from within on some February evenings. KYLIE CHAPPELL

Enough snow must have accumulated in the basin above it, and the current temperature must be warm enough to send a slender but substantial flow of meltwater as much as 1,325 feet long over the cliff. Then, Horsetail Fall bursts into a thread of fiery yellows and oranges that pulses and glows for only a few precious minutes before fading away. The sight is accompanied by the sound of cheers and sighs and the clicking of camera shutters.

Those who are old enough might have witnessed the original firefall in Yosemite's earlier days. Every evening just after dark, a huge pile of bark from the stately red firs near Glacier Point was set ablaze. After an elaborate ceremony of ritual calls between Glacier Point and the valley, the glowing coals were slowly raked over the cliff to form a fiery "waterfall" in the dark. It was a beautiful and popular tradition but more suited to an amusement park than to Yosemite, and the destruction of the natural environment was undeniable, so it was discontinued in 1968. Glowing Horsetail Fall, presented by Mother Nature herself, is infinitely more exciting today.

Miles and Directions

There are several spots around the valley floor where you can see Horsetail Fall during the day. You can start from anywhere on the Valley Loop Trail, from pullouts on Northside and Southside Roads and from several of the valley's meadows, so miles and directions vary.

19 Royal Arch Cascade

The Royal Arch Cascade flows only during a brief period of springtime snowmelt or just after a rain, but it is part of one of the most interesting and unusual settings of all the Yosemite Valley falls. The sliding water forms a pattern of shining, irregularly parallel streams that flow down the western edge of a series of enormous curved negative spaces called the Royal Arches. The whole composition is topped by the rounded crown of the Washington Column. The falling water drops a very long 1,250 feet, emerging from dense forest above, disappearing into dense forest below. Even though the falls can't compete with some of the valley's more flamboyant attractions, they do draw your attention to the beautiful pattern of this part of the valley's wall you might not notice otherwise. If you want a closer look, you can walk right up to the base of the falls as they slide over the convex granite face to temporarily flood a bit of the Valley Loop Trail just outside the Majestic (Ahwahnee) Hotel's valet parking lot.

This fall doesn't get much direct sun, so look for it at any time of day.

Height of fall: 1,250 feet
Start: Majestic (Ahwahnee) Hotel
Distance: Varies
Hiking time: A few minutes
Elevation change: Negligible
Difficulty: Easy

Seasons: Spring or any time after a hard rain
Nearest facilities: Ahwahnee (Majestic) Hotel or Curry (Half Dome) Village
Permits: None
Maps: USGS Half Dome, but no map is necessary

Finding the trailhead: You can follow the Valley Loop Trail from almost anyplace around the valley floor, or take the free shuttle bus to the Ahwahnee (Majestic) Hotel (stop 3). Wander northward through the parking lot to the entrance of the valet parking area where the Valley Loop runs past on its way to Mirror Lake. Trailhead GPS: N37 55.51' / W119 34.22'

The Hike

The whole grand panorama is best seen from the south side of the valley in front of Curry (Half Dome) Village or from Stoneman Meadow, but if you want to get personal with these beautiful cascades, you can follow the Valley Loop Trail from any direction until you come to the (Majestic) Ahwahnee Hotel. One or several of the major streams from the Royal Arch Cascade flows right next to the entrance to the hotel's valet parking lot. At high water you might have to rock-hop over a flooded section of the trail to keep your feet dry. Most of the cascade is hidden behind trees,

The Royal Arch Cascade is almost always in shade, a challenge for photographers.

The Royal Arch Cascade flows very close to the Ahwahnee (Majestic Yosemite) Hotel.

but to get closer, watch for a small brown sign with a picture of a carabiner on it that indicates the base of a climber's route. This points to a faint trail that leads steeply uphill for a very few minutes to the base of the cliff, where you can admire the patterns the water makes as it slides over the slick rock.

20 Basket Dome Fall

This waterfall is one of the most unusual and beautiful in Yosemite Valley, but it's one of Yosemite's ephemerals and you might have to make several visits before you get to see it in action. Fortunately, it's a feature of one of the valley's easiest and most popular hikes, and once you're past the first mile where most people stop, at Mirror Lake, it's less crowded than most valley locations. It is partly a cascade, partly free-falling. It flows down a notch between Basket Dome and North Dome, slides over a slight convexity, then drapes itself over a hollow space in the granite cliff like a beaded curtain hiding a mysterious room. The space behind the waterfall isn't deep, but during early spring when the snow above is melting, or just after a rainstorm, you can't really tell what might be back there. The accompanying photo is what you will see most of the time. This is an exceptionally pretty place to snowshoe during the winter, and a warm winter day is the very best time to see this waterfall.

Height of fall: Indeterminate
Start: Mirror Lake Trailhead, shuttle stop 17
Distance: 4.6-mile loop
Hiking time: 3 hours
Elevation change: 100 feet
Difficulty: Easy

Seasons: Late winter, early spring, or after a summer rainstorm
Nearest facilities: Everything you need in Yosemite Village. Toilets only at the trailhead.
Permits: None
Maps: USGS Half Dome and Yosemite Falls quads, but any free maps from the NPS will do

Finding the trailhead: Ride the Yosemite Valley shuttle bus from anyplace in the valley and get off at Mirror Lake (stop 17). Trailhead GPS: N37 44.22' / W119 33.35'

The Hike

To hike the loop in a clockwise direction, skirting the west shore of Tenaya Creek and Mirror Lake and returning along the eastern shore, follow the sign to Mirror Lake along a paved road (no longer in use except for bicycles). The trail to the right is the way you will be returning. For now, keep left along the road passing through a quiet forest of ponderosa pine, white fir, Douglas fir, incense cedar, and dogwood. At 1.0 mile the forest opens to reveal quiet Mirror Lake, reflecting Mount Watkins above it. There are sandy beaches for picnicking and wading, and the majority of visitors stop here. But if you continue on upstream, you will discover one of the more isolated, tranquil corners of Yosemite Valley, along with a chance to view a waterfall almost nobody knows about.

The trail is higher above Tenaya Creek on this side, so you can see the cliff well on the opposite side. Just a few yards after you have turned the corner, keep an eye out across to the west side of Tenaya Canyon. On your side the going can be a little

Wait for a heavy winter or heavy summer storm to see Basket Dome Fall flow.

sloppy after rain or snowmelt, but the sloppier it is, the better chance you'll have to see Basket Dome Fall in action. Watch for the bulging dome to the left, Basket Dome itself; immediately to the right of that is a gully, and farther back and a little more to the right is North Dome. (In fact, the hiking trail from Tioga Road to North Dome follows the upper part of this gully for a short distance.) Beneath the slightly bulging "forehead" of Basket Dome is a concave space, not really deep enough to be called a cave (a form granite rarely takes) but deep and dark enough that when water flows over the brow of Basket Dome, it spreads as it drops over the opening in the rock to make a filmy curtain, hiding a secret place from the outside world. It is a very unusual configuration for a Yosemite waterfall to have.

The waterfall remains in view as your trail passes a section of forest whose trees have been knocked flat by the air blast from the Ahwiyah Point rockslide. Look up to see the white spot where the darker lichen-covered rock broke loose and left a clean scar beneath. Here you must pick your way over a reconstructed trail over the rubble that crosses the base of the rockslide that kept this trail closed from 2009 to

◀ *Basket Dome Fall flows rarely but is worth waiting for.*

2012. There are a few more places off the trail where you can approach Mirror Lake from the east side if you have also come for a swim, but they are often swampy, and the trail on the west shore is a more convenient approach to the lakeside. The trail continues through fairly deep forest until it joins the road at the Tenaya Creek bridge, turns left, and heads back toward the shuttle stop.

Miles and Directions

0.0 Mirror Lake Trailhead shuttle stop 17

0.5 Road and trail split; keep left on the road

1.0 West end of Mirror Lake

2.1 Footbridge over Tenaya Creek at the far end of the trail

2.3 Views across the Tenaya Lake canyon of Basket Dome and its waterfall, if you're lucky

4.6 Arrive back at Mirror Lake Trailhead

Waterfalls of the
Western Foothills

These are waterfalls to visit when you hunger for some wilderness rambling and long for the sound of falling water as early as March and April when the high country is still icy and inaccessible. All of these cascades are between about 3,000 and 5,000 feet in elevation, where chaparral gives way to ponderosa pine and incense cedar forests in some places, beautiful old oak woodlands in others, and where the earliest of the spring wildflowers begin to bloom. None of these falls are as tall as the world-record-holding cataracts of Yosemite Valley, but every one of them is worth a visit. The approach to some of these falls along CA 41 was blackened by the 2018 Ferguson Fire, but the falls continue to flow and the upper twists and turns of the stream are more visible and even more interesting.

California poppies carpet the foothills in spring.

Rare species of flowers thrive in Ackerson Meadow.

Some of these cascades and falls lie just outside the park borders along the main routes (CA 41, CA 120, and CA 140) into Yosemite, though their sources are mostly inside the park. They are unknown to most regular Yosemite visitors who don't start looking for or thinking about waterfalls until they have crossed the park boundary, so you have a better chance to enjoy these in solitude. These spots are well known to locals, however, so weekdays before school is out are the best times to go.

Foothill vegetation springs into life in April.

21 Red Rock Falls

This short hike to a pretty little fall begins at a tiny settlement called Sugar Pine. It's less than a mile downstream from the northern trailhead of the Lewis Creek Trail. The entire trail is only 3.7 miles long with an elevation change of only about 900 feet but was added to the National Recreation Trails System in 1982 because of its beauty and historical interest. It's the setting of a flume that floated logs from the Madera–Sugar Pine Lumber Mill down to the Central Valley of California from 1900 until the Great Depression. It can be combined with the hike up from Corlieu Falls downstream, or you can hike the two falls separately. They are described separately here because to go from one fall to the other, you have to cross the creek once on a bridge that is washed out, and again on a log that is wet and slippery when the water is high (or might be washed away). The rock isn't particularly red, and the fall isn't huge, but it is very pretty and easy to get to, with lots of flowers and lovely pools. If the water level is high, there is a miniature waterwheel at the top.

It's very popular with locals from nearby communities but unknown to many Yosemite regulars. Just a few steps from the main road into Yosemite, it will feed your waterfall craving especially in spring when the higher country is still under snow.

Height of falls: 30 feet
Start: Upper Lewis Creek Trailhead
Distance: 0.8 mile out and back
Hiking time: Under an hour
Elevation change: 100 feet

Difficulty: Easy
Season: Spring to early summer
Nearest facilities: Oakhurst and Fish Camp
Permits: None for a day hike
Maps: Fish Camp

Finding the trailhead: From central Oakhurst on CA 41, drive 5 to 6 miles eastward to Sugar Pine road on the right. The road forks immediately. Follow the left fork and drive the paved road (with lots of potholes toward the end) to the hamlet of Sugar Pine, about 0.7 mile. There are only a few parking spots beside the road. A sign on the right says "Lewis Creek Trail 21E06." Trailhead GPS: N31 26.31' / W19 38.02'

The Hike

Just before you reach the hamlet of Sugar Pine, park and begin climbing gently up the signed Lewis Creek Trail above Lewis Creek mostly under cover of lovely old oaks, lined with wildflowers. The trail eventually follows the creek downstream past a series of pretty cascades. About 0.4 mile down, a side trail cuts off to the right to the top of Red Rock Falls, which flows in interesting patterns over a smooth outcrop at the base of a little pool. You will have to descend a second side trail a little farther on to get the best view of the falls. They are not big, but they free-fall over a "cliff" that

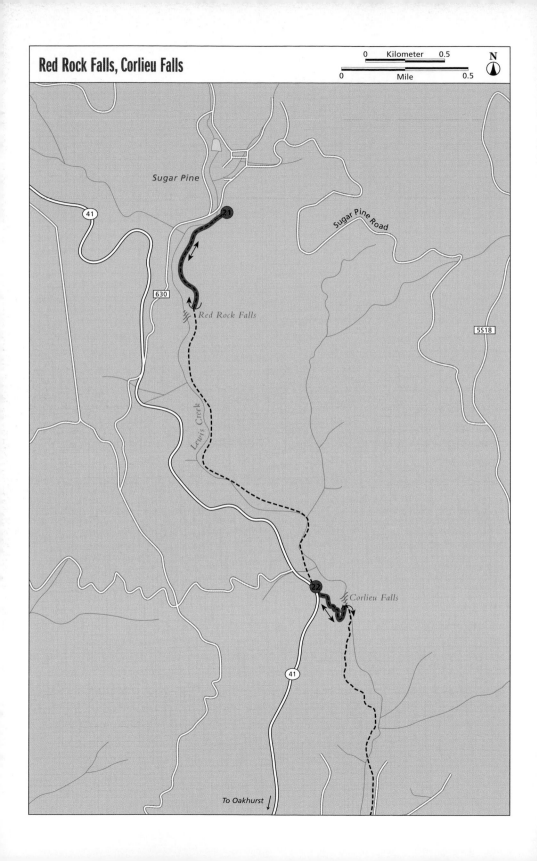

Red Rock Falls, Corlieu Falls

Sugar Pine

41

Sugar Pine Road

630

5S18

Red Rock Falls

Lewis Creek

21

22

Corlieu Falls

41

To Oakhurst

Red Rock Falls is a favorite of locals in summer.

Lewis Creek drops over Red Rock Falls in interesting patterns.

crosses the entire stream. Small but beautiful, this fall is quite different from Corlieu Falls a mile downstream on Lewis Creek.

Miles and Directions

0.0 Upper Lewis Creek Trailhead
0.3 Side trail toward Lewis Creek; turn right downhill to top of Red Rock Falls
0.4 Return to main trail. Turn right again downhill to base of Red Rock Falls.
0.8 Arrive back at the trailhead

22 Corlieu Falls

Corlieu is Madera County's highest fall at 80 feet. It may not be big, but it's so exceptionally pretty and the setting is so perfect, it's worth making a stop on your way into Yosemite if you come via CA 41. It's very popular with locals from nearby communities but unknown to many Yosemite regulars. It is just a few steps from the main road and will feed your waterfall craving in spring when the higher country is still under snow.

Corlieu Falls and Red Rock Falls are the two main attractions on the Lewis Creek Trail. The entire trail is only 3.7 miles long with an elevation change of only about 900 feet but has been added to the National Recreation Trails System because of its beauty as well as its historical interest. It is shaded by big old oak trees and dogwoods, perfumed by patches of western azaleas, and lined with the ferny leaves and delicate white blossoms of the shrub known as kit-kit-dizze (also known as mountain misery). The Lewis Creek Trail was the setting of a flume that floated logs from the Madera–Sugar Pine Lumber Mill, located upstream, to the Central Valley of California from 1900 until the Great Depression. The fall is named for Charles Corlieu, logger, rancher, and resort owner from the turn of the twentieth century.

The second waterfall, Red Rock Falls, is located not far upstream on this same trail, and many hikers do take in both falls (if not the entire Lewis Creek Trail) on the same hike. Red Rock Falls is described as a separate hike, however, partly because it requires an awkward car shuttle or a steep climb up and back down again (or vice versa). Unless the water is low enough to wade during the summer season, there are two creek crossings along the way that are frequently washed out. If you are here to see both waterfalls, your best bet is to begin at different trailheads.

Height of falls: 80 feet at the steepest part
Start: Signed Lewis Creek Trailhead
Distance: 0.6 mile out and back
Hiking time: Less than an hour of continuous walking out and back, but you will be stopping often
Elevation change: 200 feet (the whole trail is about 900 feet top to bottom, but this trail starts in the middle)

Difficulty: Moderate. Distance is short, grade is very steep.
Seasons: Spring, summer, fall
Nearest facilities: Oakhurst and Fish Camp
Permits: None for a day hike
Maps: USGS White Chief Mountain and Fish Camp quads

Finding the trailhead: From the south, on CA 41 drive through the town of Oakhurst and continue on for about 7 miles to a rather inconspicuous parking area on the right. There is a small sign on the highway on the right, just before the turnout, but it's easy to miss. There are almost always cars parked there. You will see a slightly larger sign for the Lewis Creek Trail when you are facing the creek. Just a few yards north (left) is a dirt road with another sign reading "Lewis Creek Trail 21E06." This is your trailhead. Trailhead GPS: N37 24.98' / W119 57.58'. If you're coming from Yosemite, the trailhead is 39 miles from the park entrance.

The Hike

Lots of people scramble directly downhill toward the sound of the creek from the parking area, but it's slippery and dangerous and causes lots of unnecessary erosion. Follow the road on the left downhill for just a few yards, passing a closed gate to a junction where another sign directs you to the right. As you descend the steep switchbacks, you pass a few frustratingly small openings in the trees where you can get only glimpses of the creek, but be patient. In about 0.2 mile you reach a small open viewing platform where you can get a look at the steepest point at the top of the falls, but not much more.

Below the platform Lewis Creek twists and turns so frequently that you are sure the next corner will reveal the main waterfall, top to bottom, but that doesn't happen, and you might be tempted to take shortcuts down one of the many use trails to get closer. Most of these are dangerous, go nowhere, and contribute to further erosion of the hillside. In just a few more minutes, at mile 0.3, you reach an opening in the oak forest where you will find yourself at the base of a long and exquisite cascade where the water takes multiple routes over and down and between sculptural arrangements of boulders in the most aesthetically pleasing patterns possible. There is a pool for swimming and smooth rounded rocks for basking, and from which you can look upstream to see what looks like an infinite regress of cascades.

The trail does continue farther down the gorge, and the fishing is said to be good in the pools there, though the trail becomes much steeper. If you came for the waterfalls, you have seen the best. It's a short, steep grunt back up to the parking lot.

Miles and Directions

0.0 Corlieu Falls Trailhead on the Lewis Creek Trail
0.3 Corlieu Falls
0.6 Arrive back at the trailhead

◀ *Corlieu Falls is popular with people from local communities.*

23 Foresta Falls

Crane Creek runs a long way from near Crane Flat at 6,200 feet all the way to the Merced River near El Portal, at about 2,000 feet, in a series of falls and cascades. Foresta Falls is the biggest, most impressive, and most accessible of these. The Foresta area has suffered from several extensive fires over the years, and much of the surrounding forest is gone, but there is still a fine crop of fire-following wildflowers blooming among charred conifers in spring, and Foresta Falls will help to satisfy your waterfall craving while the high country is still under snow.

Height of falls: 200 feet above the bridge with more cascades below
Start: 100 yards past the end of the pavement of Foresta Road
Distance: 1.8 miles out and back
Hiking time: 1 hour
Elevation change: 300 feet

Difficulty: Easy, steep, but short
Seasons: Spring and early summer
Nearest facilities: None at the trailhead; food, water, toilets, gas at El Portal
Permits: None
Maps: El Portal

Finding the trailhead: The Foresta Road cuts off from the Big Oak Flat Road 7 miles south of Crane Flat. Drive 1.7 miles on the paved Foresta Road to an obvious Y junction marked by a bulletin board, where you keep left. In about 2 miles a sign announces that the road is closed ahead. There is no gate blocking the road but the pavement ends. You can continue on the dirt road for another 50 to 100 yards to a wide space on the left for two or three cars. Park here. The dirt road does continue on down all the way to the bridge over the falls, but do not attempt to drive farther; the road becomes impassible and there is nowhere to turn around. Trailhead GPS: N37 41.40' / W119 45.36'

The Hike

Your goal is the abandoned bridge over the waterfall on Crane Creek. The hike begins near the creek, where there are several pretty pools and cascades just a short scramble down to the left of the road. For the main attraction, follow the road as it heads away from the creek in what looks like the wrong direction, but then makes a hairpin turn to the left and deposits you on the derelict bridge crossing the creek at its finest viewpoint. Downstream below the bridge the stream continues on its tumultuous way down to the Merced River. If you can't resist exploring further to discover what Crane Creek will do next, you can follow the old road for another 7 miles all the way to El Portal (but you will have to toil up a long, hot climb back up to your car, unless you have arranged a shuttle down on CA 140).

Foresta Falls is a favorite with residents of the settlement of Foresta. ▶

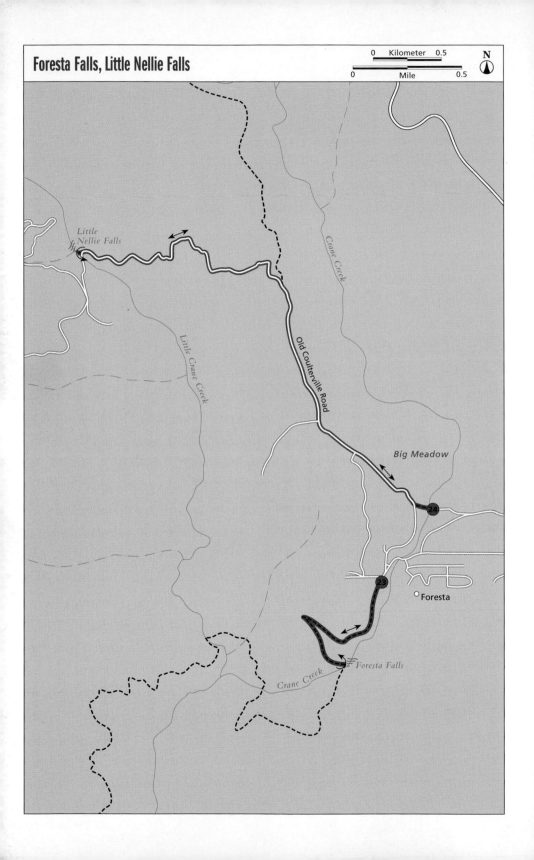

Foresta Falls, Little Nellie Falls

Little
Nellie Falls

Crane Creek

Little Crane Creek

Old Coulterville Road

Big Meadow

24

23

Foresta

Crane Creek

Foresta Falls

0   Kilometer   0.5

0   Mile   0.5

N

The forest around Foresta has suffered repeated burns.

Crane Creek makes several cascades and falls on its way to the Merced River.

Foresta Falls takes its first of a series of steps on the way to the Merced River.

Miles and Directions

0.0 Small parking area just past the end of the pavement of Foresta Road

0.9 Bridge over Foresta Falls on Crane Creek

1.8 Arrive back at the trailhead

24 Little Nellie Falls

This is a good springtime hike to a cool green oasis tucked into the brushy, summer-dry western foothills of the Sierra, especially when the high country of Yosemite is still under snow. Little Nellie Falls tumble down Little Crane Creek until it joins (Big) Crane Creek on its way to the Merced River. The trail follows the historic Old Coulterville Road, the first wagon road into Yosemite, completed in 1874 but abandoned not long afterward. The area near Big Meadow has seen periodic fires that have created good habitat for fields of wildflowers in spring. The falls are a favorite with local residents, but few Yosemite visitors know about it, so it's a good choice for those who treasure solitude.

Height of falls: Indeterminate, many cascades along Little Crane Creek, but the fall just above the crossing is 40 feet
Start: Ruined bridge blocking the Old Coulterville Road beyond the old barn at Foresta
Distance: 5.4 miles out and back
Hiking time: 3 to 4 hours
Elevation change: 600 feet
Difficulty: Easy

Seasons: All year, but best in spring and early summer
Nearest facilities: Food, water, phone, toilet, and gas at El Portal
Permits: None
Maps: El Portal
Special considerations: There is no shade or water along this old road until you get almost all the way to the falls, and it can be very hot in summer. Carry plenty of water.

Finding the trailhead: The Foresta Road cuts off from the Big Oak Flat Road about 7 miles south of Crane Flat. Drive 1.7 miles on the paved Foresta Road to an obvious Y intersection with a bulletin board. Keep right. The road leaves blacktop here and passes an old barn on the edge of Big Meadow. In another 0.2 mile the road ends in front of a green house at a washed-out bridge. This is your trailhead, with room for several cars. GPS: N37 42.11' / W119 45.10'

The Hike

Cross the creek on a bridge that is safe for humans but too rickety for cars. The closed old road climbs gently through brush, and if you glance back to the right, you will eventually get a glimpse of El Capitan and Half Dome off to the east, then lose them as the road makes a dip.

Pass a junction with an unmarked road that cuts off to the left. A short distance later you will see a second junction on the left with a crude sign that says "Flying Spur." Pass by that one too. The road soon enters, then very shortly leaves, Yosemite Park. At mile 2 cross over a low rise as the road forks again where a gate blocks the right fork. This time you do take the left fork. Now you will find yourself on the

A memorial sign welcoming hunters places Little Nellie just outside the park.

Little Nellie Falls provide a refreshing oasis in summer.

Half Dome and El Capitan can be seen from Yosemite's foothills.

moist side of the hill, where early season trickles begin to appear. Don't be disappointed by the first minor cascade you see. Little Nellie is still ahead. Walk downhill to another, smaller gate that marks the entrance back into Yosemite. In 0.3 mile find a sign and a final gate leaving the park. Just beyond is a picnic table and Little Nellie.

Miles and Directions

0.0 Closed road at Big Meadow

2.7 Little Nellie Falls

5.4 Arrive back at the trailhead

25 Preston Falls

This is a little-known treasure. Even most longtime Yosemite regulars have never heard of it, but it's one of the very finest springtime hikes anywhere, with lots of variety and lots of solitude. It follows the Middle Fork of the Tuolumne River in the Stanislaus National Forest right on Yosemite's border. You hike along cascade after cascade to wind up at a very pretty pool fed by a multilevel waterfall. The show of springtime wildflowers rivals that of any of the other natural garden spots around Yosemite you've visited. The catch is that your timing is critical. The trail starts at only 2,800 feet and doesn't gain much elevation, so by late spring or early summer, it's much too hot and dry and loses its charm.

Height of falls: About 30 feet
Start: Stanislaus National Forest Trailhead
Distance: 8.2 miles out and back
Hiking time: 4–5 hours, allow all day
Elevation change: 540 feet
Difficulty: Moderate
Seasons: Apr, May

Nearest facilities: Food, phone, gas at Buck Meadows. Outhouse, no potable water at trailhead.
Permits: None for a day hike, wilderness permits not required, but you do need a fire permit if you plan to have a fire
Maps: Cherry Lake South
Special considerations: Poison oak and rattlesnakes, both easy to avoid if you stay alert

Finding the trailhead: Drive about 14 miles west on CA 120 from the Big Oak Flat entrance to Yosemite to the Cherry Lake turnoff on the right. Follow the steep winding road, also known as Road 17, downhill for 10 miles, crossing the Middle Fork of the Tuolumne River on a bridge at the bottom. Turn right and pass carefully thorough a tiny hamlet housing workers and their families on the dam. The trailhead is 0.8 mile beyond, marked by a sign that says "Stanislaus National Forest Trailhead." There is a pit toilet but nothing else. GPS: N37 52.718' / W119 57.031'

The Hike

Start at the trailhead beside the outhouse that says "Stanislaus National Forest Trailhead." It doesn't say anything about Preston Falls. Maybe that's a good thing. The beginning and a few other spots along the trail are rough and rocky as it rises and falls along the streamside where the walls are close together. At times where there is room, the trail wanders through flat meadows, then when the walls close again, you find yourself scrambling above the roar of the river. There are lots of shady oaks and wildflowers from the start, and there are several good campsites along the way. The final mile of trail wanders over flat ground beside the river running dark green, deep, and quiet until at last you hear the sound of moving water from a series of unexcep-

Preston Falls

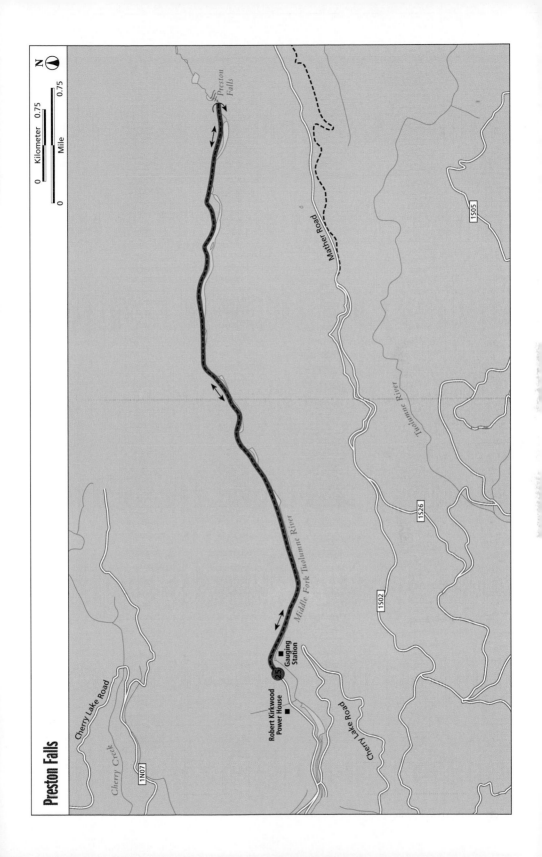

The Middle Fork of the Tuolumne River flows over Preston Falls.

tional but enthusiastic—and very welcome—waterfalls. It is such a beautiful hike, it's a wonder this trail isn't more heavily used.

Miles and Directions

- **0.0** Stanislaus National Forest Trailhead
- **0.3** Pass a gauging station on other (south) side of the river
- **2.6** Begin final open section of trail out of sight of the river
- **4.1** Reach Preston Falls
- **8.2** Arrive back at the trailhead

Wawona-Area Falls

The Wawona area is relatively low in elevation (5,000 to 6,000 feet), and though it is higher than the floor of Yosemite Valley, it lacks the glacial history and the extreme topography of hanging valleys and vertical cliffs that make lots of big waterfalls. Still, Wawona does have two very impressive waterfalls that you won't want to miss, especially since they are tucked away in corners of the park that fewer visitors see. Both of them flow all year, and both require moderate to strenuous uphill hiking. They are perfect for late-spring and early-summer hikes or backpacks when the high country is under snow and creek crossings are dangerous.

Wawona is the site of a historical overnight stage stop on the way to Yosemite Valley just off CA 41, about 4 miles into the park. It's above the western foothills in a mixed forest of ponderosa and sugar pine, white fir, Douglas fir, and incense cedar. It was subject to logging in the past, along with periodic prescribed (and occasional unprescribed) fires followed by explosions of wildflowers.

There is a Pioneer History Center, the Wawona (aka Big Trees) Hotel, a campground, a small store, gas station . . . and a golf course! There is a wilderness office next to the hotel where you can get a wilderness permit if you plan to backpack to or beyond the waterfalls. Just beyond is North Wawona, a little settlement with a store and cottages, some for rent. It is a private inholding (private property surrounded by national park).

The Wawona area's claim to fame is the Mariposa Grove of giant sequoias.

26 Alder Creek Falls

Very few people know about this special place outside of Yosemite Valley. It's a great early season hike for wildflower lovers in spring through a quiet and infrequently traveled section of the park. There are no high peaks or grand vistas, but the route passes through a variety of habitats, from chaparral through oak woodland to pine and fir forest, culminating at a surprisingly tall and truly enchanting waterfall.

Height of falls: 100 feet
Start: Alder Creek Trailhead at Mosquito Creek
Distance: 7.8 miles out and back
Hiking time: 4–5 hours
Elevation change: 1,500 feet
Difficulty: Moderate
Seasons: Spring and fall. The falls run year-round, but summer can be hot.

Nearest facilities: Food, water, toilets, gas at Wawona
Permits: None for a day hike
Maps: Wawona
Special considerations: Watch for rattlesnakes in the thick brush.

Finding the trailhead: Drive CA 41 about 4 miles north of Wawona on the right (east) side of the road to Mosquito Creek. The sign may be missing, but you'll see a small parking area with two bear boxes on the west side of the street. If you miss it, about a mile beyond Mosquito Creek, you'll find a sign, also on the right, marked "Alder Creek." This is not the trailhead. The trail begins at Mosquito Creek on the right side of the road across from the bear boxes. Trailhead GPS: N37 34.31' / W119 40.46'

The Hike

You probably won't be able to see the trailhead from your car, but it's obvious when you walk across the road and spot a sign a short distance up the trail. Begin your climb through a rapidly recovering fire-scarred grove of ponderosa pines and black oaks, dense with ceanothus and elderberry bushes heavy with fruit in late spring. Watch where you step in the first section of this trail since the brush is thick enough to hide rattlesnakes, who will make every effort to get out of your way but will probably bite you if you step on them. At a junction 0.7 mile along, the brush becomes patchier. Your route turns sharply to the left (east) and continues to climb. The right fork heads back toward Wawona.

Soon the way levels out and you contour through more open forest, crossing little flowery seeps early in the season.

At about 3 miles the trail becomes an abandoned railroad bed, used by the Sugar Pine Lumber Company to cut and haul away most of the big old–growth sugar pines in the region. Within a few minutes you will begin to hear the falls ahead. Round a corner and the entire waterfall from top to bottom appears. You may be tempted

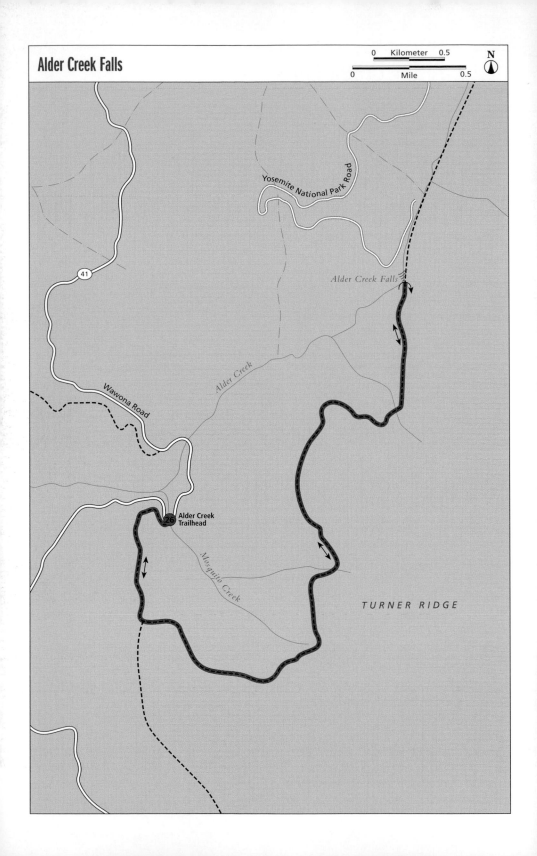

Alder Creek Falls

0 Kilometer 0.5
0 Mile 0.5

N

41

Yosemite National Park Road

Alder Creek Falls

Wawona Road

Alder Creek

26 Alder Creek Trailhead

Mosquito Creek

TURNER RIDGE

Alder Creek Falls are one of Yosemite's least-visited falls.

Rattlers must seek shelter to keep cool on hot days.

to slide and scramble down the slope to the base of the falls, but it is very steep and unstable. Enjoy it from your perfect viewpoint above. Continue along the road and finally reach upper Alder Creek above the falls, crossing little tributary creeks in spring. You can continue along the creek for miles and will see lots of tempting camping spots, all of which are much too close to the water to be legal.

Return the way you came.

Miles and Directions

0.0 Alder Creek Trailhead at Mosquito Creek

0.7 Trail junction; turn sharp left

3.0 Trail becomes road

3.9 Top of Alder Creek Falls

7.8 Arrive back at the trailhead

27 Chilnualna Falls

Chilnualna Creek seldom flows slowly, instead tumbling in cascades and free-falling almost constantly for most of its length. The most spectacular sections and highest waterfalls are found at the beginning and end of the hike, and the trail has been built so that it comes closest to the creek at those spots. You can take a short, steep climb right alongside the wildest, most riotous section, then return to the trailhead. It's a steady, uphill pull all the way to the top, but the grade is comfortable. This fall would be much more frequently visited if it were not tucked away in a little corner of Yosemite. It is as exciting as any in Yosemite Valley, and used to be almost unknown but is rapidly becoming popular.

Height of falls: 690 feet to 2,200 feet depending on what you measure
Start: Chilnualna Falls Trailhead
Distance: 8.2 miles out and back; 0.4 mile out and back to the lower fall
Hiking time: 6–8 hours or overnight or 40 minutes to the lower fall
Elevation change: 4,200 feet, 200 feet to the lower fall
Difficulty: Moderate; it's short but all uphill
Seasons: Spring, early summer, and fall; midsummer is hot, fall is pleasant, but the water is low

Nearest facilities: Food, gas, and phones in North Wawona
Permits: None for a day hike; available for overnights in advance or at Wawona Visitor Center
Maps: USGS Wawona and Mariposa Grove quads
Special considerations: Watch for rattlesnakes in this low-elevation area. They are not aggressive but do not like to be handled or stepped on.

Finding the trailhead: From CA 41 turn right (east) on Chilnualna Road and continue on through Wawona, then through the little village of North Wawona for 2 miles to a signed parking lot on the right. The trailhead is on the left. Trailhead GPS: N37 32.53' / W119 38.09'

The Hike

Follow the trail signs from the parking lot and cross the paved road. Another sign routes horse traffic to the left and foot traffic to the right. The footpath, much too rugged for horses, heads steeply up, sometimes on big granite stairsteps right beside the roaring water, then cuts away from the stream where the horse and foot trails rejoin in 0.2 mile at a big sign. Long, wide switchbacks make the northward climb almost painless. The forest floor is covered with a solid carpet of the white shrub called kit-kit-dizze under oak, pine, and incense cedar. At about a mile the trail switchbacks to a point near the creek, then climbs out of reach of water until very near the end of the hike, except for little tributary streams that are reliable only in early season. As you gain height, more of Chilnualna's upper fall comes into view

Chilnualna Falls

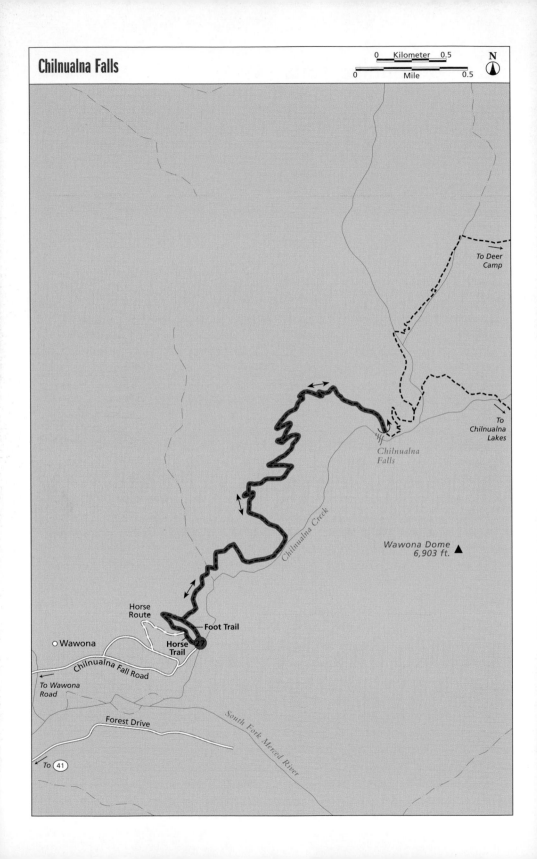

0   Kilometer   0.5

0   Mile   0.5

N

To Deer Camp

To Chilnualna Lakes

Chilnualna Falls

Chilnualna Creek

Wawona Dome
6,903 ft. ▲

Horse Route

Foot Trail

○ Wawona

Horse Trail

27

Chilnualna Fall Road

To Wawona Road

South Fork Merced River

Forest Drive

To 41

The trail climbs close beside the lower section of Chilnualna Falls.

Chilnualna Creek has worn deep potholes into the granite creek bed.

behind clouds of rising mist. When the trail approaches the elevation of the falls, it rounds a ridge blasted out of the rock by dynamite and deposits you right beside the thundering cataract. Brilliant magenta mountain pride penstemon line cracks in the streamside rocks. From here you can see all the way back down to Wawona Meadow.

Climb a few more hot and brushy switchbacks until the trail emerges onto slabs of classic exfoliating Yosemite granite to an even more dramatic section of the falls. The smooth rock near the water invites exploration, but move carefully as the rocks are slippery and it's a long way down. A sign at the trail junction tells you that it is 5.6 miles back to Wawona, but that is the distance to the ranger station where the trailhead used to be, not to the closer one where you began. Return the way you came.

Miles and Directions

0.0 Chilnualna Falls Trailhead; keep right at horse/foot trail split

0.2 Horse and foot trails rejoin; continue uphill

1.0 Trail is nearest the creek

4.1 Chilnualna Falls

8.2 Arrive back at Chilnualna Falls Trailhead

Waterfalls in the Heart of the Park

Most of the waterfalls in this region require an overnight backpacking or mule-packing journey unless you are in such extraordinary physical condition that you can cover many rugged miles at high elevation in a single day.

The high mountain country includes falls and cascades along the Merced River, one of the two biggest and most important rivers (along with the Tuolumne) in Yosemite, and it's the one that flows through Yosemite Valley. That means that the majority of visitors to Yosemite are familiar with its most famous features, Vernal Fall and Nevada Fall. But there are many more marvelous falls and cascades upstream if you're willing to expend a little more effort to see them. The Merced originates

The Cathedral Lakes are one of the most popular destinations in the heart of Yosemite.

May Lake is the site of one of Yosemite's popular High Sierra Camps.

in the Clark Range, where a number of tributaries—the Triple Peak Fork, Merced Fork, Lyell Peak Fork, Red Peak Fork, and Grey Peak Fork—join one after another around Merced and Washburn Lakes. Its length is estimated to be between 80 and 150 miles, depending on where you start counting, and it descends from about 8,000 feet to 900 feet where it joins the San Joaquin River below a series of dams that collect water for agriculture in the Central Valley of California.

Merced Lake High Sierra Camp and Vogelsang High Sierra Camp are two of the stops on the very popular six-day High Sierra Camp loop. (Glen Aulin High Sierra Camp, in the Grand Canyon of the Tuolumne region, is another.) The portion of this loop between the Merced Lake and Vogelsang has some of the grandest falls and cascades in the park. There are two routes between these two camps. The Fletcher Creek Trail skirts the northwest flank of Vogelsang Peak and is lower in elevation and a little shorter. The Lewis Creek Trail skirts the southeast flank of the peak and reaches an elevation of 10,700 feet at Vogelsang Pass. Vogelsang is the highest of the High Sierra Camps at 10,100 feet and might not be open as early as Merced Lake since the Tioga Road might be closed and trailheads inaccessible until snow can be cleared later in the season.

If you are lucky enough to get reservations to stay at one or more of the camps, or if you are using one of the campgrounds associated with each camp, you can explore the falls along either or both of these trails in any order you like. If your time is more limited and you must choose one or the other of these High Sierra Camps as your base, the route to each camp will be described from its nearest road head.

28 Merced River Falls

This is a spectacular cascade unnamed on the map, but it's the first big one you encounter on the Merced River above Vernal and Nevada Falls (discussed in the Yosemite Valley section). It marks the beginning of a series of such marvelous manifestations of falling water that you will probably have to adjust (downward) the number of miles you planned to cover each day. This cascade marks the upper end of Little Yosemite Valley, which was burned by the Meadow Fire in 2014. The final mile of the hike can be hot and shadeless, making the sight of this noisy, exuberant cascade all the more welcoming. Go before August if you can.

Height of falls: 65 feet
Start: Happy Isles (see "Special Considerations," below, for alternates)
Distance: 13.6 miles out and back
Hiking time: All day or overnight
Elevation change: 2,500 feet
Difficulty: Strenuous
Season: Late spring through summer
Nearest facilities: Half Dome (Curry) Village, toilets at trailhead, Vernal Fall Bridge, above Nevada Fall
Permits: Available for overnights in advance or from the wilderness center at Yosemite Village

Maps: USGS Half Dome and Merced Peak quads
Special considerations: This hike is described from the John Muir Trail beginning at Happy Isles. There is lots of competition for wilderness permits using either this route or the parallel Mist Trail route, but there are other alternative trailheads. You can start at Glacier Point and follow the Panorama Trail, or begin at Mono Meadow off the Glacier Point Road, both of which take you to the top of Nevada Fall, where the Muir Trail and the Mist Trail meet.

Finding the trailhead: Park in the hikers' lot east of Half Dome (Curry) Village and follow the well-marked trail to Happy Isles from the east end of the lot. Or you can take the shuttle bus to Happy Isles (stop 16) from anywhere in the valley. From the shuttle bus stop, continue on the paved road over the Happy Isles Bridge, then turn right, following the river upstream to the big sign that marks the beginning of the John Muir Trail. Trailhead GPS: N37 43.51' / W119 33.33'

The Hike

The big sign at the trailhead marks the beginning of the John Muir Trail, showing mileage to various points all the way to trail's end at Mount Whitney, about 211 miles to the south. Don't expect a true wilderness experience here. This is a popular spot for good reason, but the farther you go, the more solitude you'll find. The trail climbs gently through black oak and pine forest among enormous lichen-draped boulders up along the north bank of the Merced. A little spring trickles out of the rocks a few hundred yards up on your left. (*Note:* Don't drink the water here without purifying it.) The trail steepens gradually as you climb, but you'll want to stop frequently anyway to enjoy the roaring river through openings in the trees. In about a half mile,

Merced River Falls, Bunnell Cascade

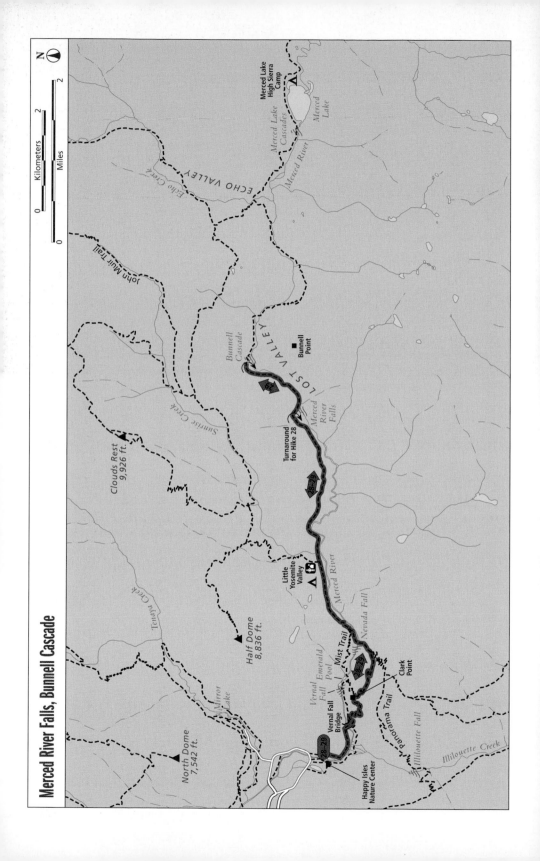

N

Kilometers
0   2

Miles
0   2

North Dome
7,542 ft.

Mirror Lake

Half Dome
8,836 ft.

Tenaya Creek

Clouds Rest
9,926 ft.

Sunrise Creek

John Muir Trail

Echo Creek

ECHO VALLEY

Merced Lake Cascades

Merced Lake High Sierra Camp

Merced Lake

Merced River

Bunnell Cascade

LOST VALLEY

Bunnell Point

Merced River Falls

Turnaround for Hike 28

28-29

62

Little Yosemite Valley

Merced River

Vernal Emerald Fall Pool

Mist Trail

Nevada Fall

28-29

Clark Point

Panorama Trail

Illilouette Fall

Illilouette Creek

Vernal Fall Bridge

28-29

Happy Isles Nature Center

The Merced River Gorge is one of the most exciting views in Yosemite.

across the Merced to your right and tucked back up in Illilouette Gorge, Illilouette Fall pours 370 feet down the Panorama Cliff to meet the Merced River. The trail descends to the bridge, which you cross at 0.8 mile for a view of 317-foot Vernal Fall upstream. (There is a toilet and water fountain here.)

In 0.2 mile the trail splits. The left fork follows the Mist Trail, but your route (safer and easier with a backpack) follows the John Muir Trail to Clark Point at 2.3 miles, where the sight of Nevada Fall rushing 594 feet into the gorge below will stop you in your tracks. This is surely one of the finest waterfall views in the world.

Continue ascending the John Muir Trail on well-graded switchbacks, passing beneath a dripping rock overhang decorated with delicate gardens of ferns, columbines, and tiny orchids tucked into the cracks. At 3.3 miles the Panorama Trail, leading back to Glacier Point, joins this one from the right. The trail drops a bit, hops a couple of little creeks, then emerges into a wide sunny expanse of granite at the top of Nevada Fall. Here, at 3.5 miles, cross the footbridge that spans the river. Please heed the warning signs and do not try to swim, wade, or ford the river. There are fatalities here almost every year. Follow the north shore of the river to a junction with the upper end of the Mist Trail at 3.8 miles, marked by an outhouse. Continue upstream, climbing the well-defined trail over inlaid rocks. The way soon passes from sunlight into shade, and the Merced changes from a raging torrent to become quiet, dark, and deep.

At 4.3 miles ignore a turnoff to Half Dome on the left, and hike on to Little Yosemite Valley at 4.8 miles. It's a busy place, especially for bears. If you plan to spend the night there, a ranger will be checking your wilderness permit and making sure you have a bear canister. Be sure to admire the architecturally elegant two-story composting outhouse too. The National Park Service has constructed two communal fire rings for campers to share. Please do not scar this already overused area by building another one.

This is your last camping opportunity for at least the next 2 miles since camping is prohibited for 2 miles beyond the campground. Little Yosemite Valley is not an inviting place since the 2014 Meadow Fire anyway. Your next section of trail seems a relentless, shadeless collection of black stumps. If you arrive early enough in the summer, you do have a new opportunity to see several of the ephemeral waterfalls pouring down the cliffs that used to be hidden by the forest. There is a little greenery and fire-following flowers blooming at the base of the stumps, but it will take many years for this area to recover.

By mile 6.8 the cliff walls pinch together beneath Moraine Dome to force the Merced, which has been out of sight for the last mile or so, into a gushing, glorious cascade tumbling down into the devastated valley. There is one marginally legal campsite near the fall, and there isn't much decent camping for a mile or so beyond this, so you must continue on for another mile to camp, or return to the trailhead. You can also check with the wilderness center about camping near the base of the cascade.

Miles and Directions

0.0   Happy Isles
0.8   Vernal Fall Bridge
0.9   Trail splits; turn right onto the John Muir Trail
2.3   Clark Point; keep right again on the John Muir Trail
3.3   Panorama Trail heads right; keep left toward Nevada Fall
3.5   Cross the bridge over Nevada Fall
3.8   Mist Trail joins this one at a restroom; keep right
4.3   Keep straight ahead as trail to Half Dome goes left
4.8   Little Yosemite Valley
6.8   Merced River Falls
13.6   Arrive back at Happy Isles

◀   *The depth of Merced Gorge and the volume of the river require many bridges.*

29 Bunnell Cascade

This is the second big cascade along the ascent up the Merced River, and it is usually a lively place. When the water level is right, dozens of (usually young) people find a spot partway down from the top of the fall, edge themselves into the center of the flow in a sitting position, push off, and ride the rushing waterslide 20 to 30 feet into the pool at the base. Timing is important. If the water level is too low, you're bound to lose some skin; if it's too high, the river can break your bones . . . or worse. At very high water, this cascade is sometimes run by kayakers!

Height of fall: At least 60 feet
Start: Happy Isles
Distance: 15.8 miles out and back
Hiking time: All day or overnight
Elevation change: 2,700 feet
Difficulty: Strenuous
Season: Late spring through summer
Nearest facilities: Everything you need except gas in Yosemite Valley, toilets and water at Vernal Fall Bridge, toilets above Nevada Fall Bridge
Permits: None for a day hike, available in advance or from the Yosemite Valley Wilderness Center

Maps: USGS Half Dome and Merced Peak quads
Special considerations: This hike is described using the John Muir Trail beginning at Happy Isles. There is lots of competition for wilderness permits using either this route or the parallel Mist Trail route, but there are other alternative trailheads. You can start at Glacier Point and follow the Panorama Trail, or begin at the Mono Meadow trailhead to the top of Nevada Fall, or you can begin at the Mono Meadow trailhead off the Glacier Point Road, both of which take you to the top of Nevada Fall, where the Muir Trail and the Mist Trail meet.

Finding the trailhead: Park in the hikers' lot east of Half Dome (Curry) Village and follow the well-marked trail to Happy Isles from the east end of the lot. Or you can take the free shuttle bus to Happy Isles (stop 16) from anywhere in the valley. From the shuttle bus stop, continue on the paved road over the Happy Isles Bridge, then turn right (south), following the river upstream to the big sign on the left that marks the beginning of the John Muir Trail. Trailhead GPS: N37 43.51' / W119 33.33'

The Hike

The big sign at the trailhead marks the beginning of the John Muir Trail, showing mileage to various points all the way to trail's end at Mount Whitney, about 211 miles to the south. Don't expect a true wilderness experience here. This is a popular spot for good reason, but the farther you go, the more solitude you'll find. The trail climbs gently through black oak and pine forest among enormous lichen-draped boulders up along the north bank of the Merced. A little spring trickles out of the rocks a few

An ephemeral waterfall pours into Lost Canyon.

Many hikers ride down the Bunnell Cascade slide at lower water.

hundred yards up on your left. (**Note:** Don't drink the water here without purifying it.) The trail steepens gradually as you climb, but you'll want to stop frequently anyway to enjoy the roaring river through openings in the trees. In about a half mile, across the Merced to your right and tucked back up in Illilouette Gorge, Illilouette Fall pours 370 feet down the Panorama Cliff to meet the Merced River. The trail descends to the bridge, which you cross at 0.8 mile, for a view of 317-foot Vernal Fall upstream. (There is a toilet and water fountain here.)

In 0.2 mile the trail splits. The left fork follows the Mist Trail, but your route (safer and easier with a backpack) follows the John Muir Trail to Clark Point at 2.3 miles, where the sight of Nevada Fall rushing 594 feet into the gorge below will stop you in your tracks. This is surely one of the finest waterfall views in the world.

Continue ascending the John Muir Trail on well-graded switchbacks, passing beneath a dripping rock overhang decorated with delicate gardens of ferns, columbines, and tiny orchids tucked into the cracks. At 3.3 miles the Panorama Trail, leading back to Glacier Point, joins this one from the right. The trail drops a bit, hops a couple of little creeks, then emerges into a wide sunny expanse of granite at the top of Nevada Fall. Here, at 3.5 miles, cross the footbridge that spans the river. Please heed the warning signs and do not try to swim, wade, or ford the river. There are fatalities here almost every year. Follow the north shore of the river to a junction with the upper end of the Mist Trail at 3.8 miles, marked by an outhouse. Continue upstream, climbing the well-defined trail over inlaid rocks. The way soon passes from

The rock is rough for sliding at low water in Bunnell Cascade.

sunlight into shade, and the Merced changes from a raging torrent to become quiet, dark, and deep.

At 4.3 miles ignore a turnoff to Half Dome on the left, and hike on to Little Yosemite Valley at 4.8 miles. It's a busy place, especially for bears. If you plan to spend the night there, a ranger will be checking your wilderness permit and making sure you have a bear canister. Be sure to admire the architecturally elegant two-story composting outhouse too. The National Park Service has constructed two communal fire rings for campers to share. Please do not scar this already overused area by building another one.

This is your last camping opportunity for at least the next 2 miles since camping is prohibited for 2 miles beyond the campground. Little Yosemite Valley is not an inviting place since the 2014 Meadow Fire anyway.

Your next section of trail seems a relentless, shadeless collection of black stumps. If you arrive early enough in the summer, you do have a new opportunity to see several of the ephemeral waterfalls pouring down the cliffs that used to be hidden by the forest. There is a little greenery and some fire-following flowers bloom at the base of the stumps, but it will take many years for this area to recover.

By mile 6.8 the cliff walls pinch together beneath Moraine Dome to force the Merced, which has been out of sight for the last mile or so, into a glorious, gushing cascade tumbling down into the devastated valley. There is one marginally legal campsite near the fall, and there isn't much decent camping for a mile or so beyond this, so you must continue on for another mile to camp.

In early summer the water in Bunnell Cascade is dangerous to slide.

Above the first cascade the Merced slows and widens out once again through Lost Valley, which was burned some time before the Meadow Fire. You can see it's had more time to recover since the trail takes you through a veritable jungle of shoulder-high lupines, a typical fire-following species.

The canyon walls once again squeeze together as you climb out of the valley, passing below the dome of Bunnell Point across the river above the spot where the water pours over the long, slippery slide of Bunnell Cascade. There aren't any good camping spots near Bunnell Cascade, where fire-following weedy grasses have colonized a former burn, but if you have the energy to continue another half mile or so, you'll find an opening in the forest between Lost Valley and Echo Valley with a luxurious backpackers campsite complete with log tables and chairs and a little creek flowing down to meet the Merced.

Miles and Directions

- **0.0** Happy Isles
- **0.8** Vernal Fall Bridge
- **0.9** Trail splits; turn right onto the John Muir Trail
- **2.3** Clark Point, keep right again on the JMT
- **3.3** Panorama Trail heads right; keep left toward Nevada Fall
- **3.5** Cross the bridge over Nevada Fall
- **3.8** The Mist Trail joins this one at a restroom. Continue straight ahead.
- **4.3** Keep straight ahead again as trail to Half Dome goes left
- **4.8** Little Yosemite Valley
- **6.8** Merced River Falls
- **7.9** Bunnell Point and Bunnell Cascade
- **15.8** Arrive back at Happy Isles

30 Merced Lake Cascades

The Merced River never quits. Just before you get to Merced Lake High Sierra Camp, when you're tired from your hike, the last mile or so of trail before you reach Merced Lake has the most varied and interesting set of cascades anywhere. And you're close as the trail is often beside them and you're not looking at a faraway gorge. It's the scale that is so attractive. As a bonus, you get to experience two other very enthusiastic cascades along the way, the second of which, Bunnell (if the water level is safe) offers an exciting waterslide into a little pool.

Height of fall: Indeterminate
Start: Happy Isles
Distance: 26.2 miles out and back
Hiking time: Overnight
Elevation change: 3,600 feet
Difficulty: Moderately strenuous
Season: Late spring to early fall

Nearest facilities: Half Dome (Curry) Village. Snacks, emergency supplies, toilet, water at Merced Lake High Sierra Camp.
Permits: Required for overnights in advance or from the wilderness center at Yosemite Village
Maps: USGS Half Dome and Merced Peak quads

Finding the trailhead: Park in the hikers' lot east of Half Dome (Curry) Village and follow the well-marked trail to Happy Isles from the east end of the lot. Or you can take the shuttle bus to Happy Isles (stop 16) from anywhere in the valley. From the shuttle bus stop, continue on the paved road over the Happy Isles Bridge, then turn right, following the river upstream to the big sign that marks the beginning of the John Muir Trail. Trailhead GPS: N37 43.51' / W119 33.33'

The Hike

The John Muir Trail sign shows mileage to various points all the way to trail's end at Mount Whitney, about 211 miles to the south. The first couple of miles of the John Muir Trail get so much traffic that they have been paved, but don't let that deter you from using this trailhead. It's popular for good reason.

The trail climbs gently through black oak and pine forest among enormous lichen-draped boulders up along the north bank of the Merced. A little spring trickles out of the rocks a few hundred yards up on your left. (*Note:* Don't drink the water here without purifying it.) The trail steepens gradually as you climb, but you'll want to stop frequently anyway to enjoy the roaring river through openings in the trees. In about a half mile, across the Merced canyon to your right and tucked back up in Illilouette Gorge, Illilouette Fall pours 370 feet down the Panorama Cliff to meet the Merced River. It is a big waterfall but most people miss it. If you stop now and then to glance behind you, you will find that Upper Yosemite Fall is visible too.

The trail suddenly descends to the bridge at 0.8 mile, where dozens of visitors will be taking photos or gazing in delight at 317-foot Vernal Fall upstream. There are

Merced Lake is the site of the largest of the High Sierra Camps.

restrooms, a water fountain, and dozens of freeloading, usually overweight, ground squirrels near the bridge. For their health and your safety, do not feed them.

Cross the bridge to the south side of the river and turn left (upstream). At 1.1 mile the Mist Trail stays to the left. Your route turns right on the John Muir Trail and ascends on well-graded switchbacks through shady mixed-conifer forest until you round a corner to Clark Point at mile 2.1. Here, one of the most spectacular of Yosemite's many overlooks will stop you in your tracks as Nevada Fall thunders down the canyon straight ahead in classic postcard style. The rounded shape behind and just to the left of Liberty Cap (itself just to the left of the fall) is the back side of Half Dome.

From Clark Point turn right, climb a few more switchbacks, then pass through a cut in the side of the cliff beneath a weeping rock overhang that drizzles water onto the trail. Delicate ferns, columbines, and tiny white orchids are tucked into the cracks. Begin to lose a little elevation, and at mile 3.3 pass through an open gate at a junction with the Panorama Trail. Continue left through a shady little gully where water sometimes pools deeply enough to slosh over the tops of your boots, then round a corner to emerge onto a sunny bench. At mile 3.5 cross the footbridge that spans the river. Nevada Fall crashes through an impossibly narrow notch and is visible all the way to the bottom, sometimes projecting a rainbow near the base.

Follow the north shore of the river to a junction with the upper end of the Mist Trail at 3.8 miles, marked by an outhouse. Continue upstream, climbing the well-defined trail over inlaid rocks. The way soon passes from sunlight into shade, and the Merced changes from a raging torrent to become quiet, dark, and deep.

Merced Lake Cascades

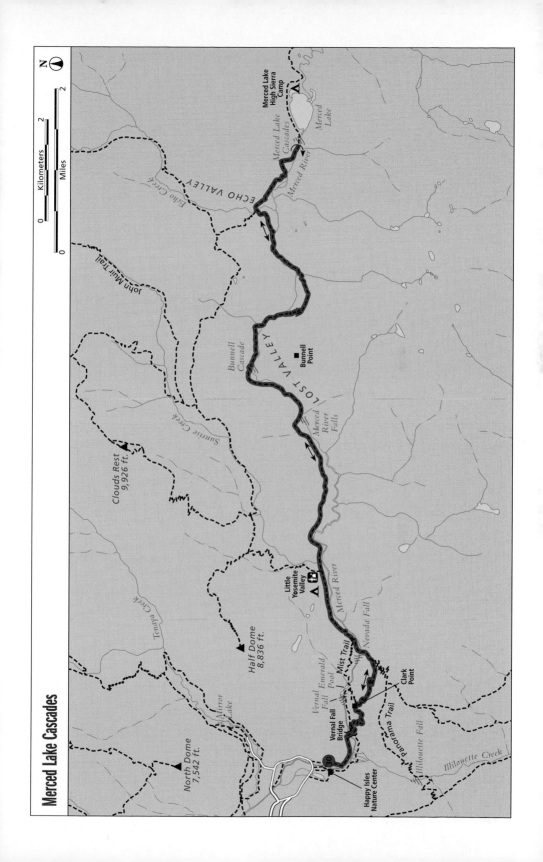

The trail often follows the Merced River through narrow gorges.

At 4.3 miles ignore a turnoff to Half Dome on the left, and hike on to Little Yosemite Valley at 4.8 miles. It's a busy place, especially for bears, and a ranger will be checking your wilderness permit and making sure you have a bear canister. Be sure to admire the architecturally elegant two-story composting outhouse too. This is your last camping opportunity for at least the next 2 miles since camping is prohibited for 2 miles beyond the campground. Little Yosemite Valley is not an inviting place since the 2014 Meadow Fire anyway. Your next section of trail seems a relentless, shadeless collection of black stumps.

By mile 6.8 the cliff walls pinch together beneath Moraine Dome to force the Merced, which has been out of sight for the last mile or so, into a gushing, glorious cascade tumbling down into the devastated valley. There isn't much decent camping for another mile or so after this.

Above this first cascade the Merced slows and widens out once again through Lost Valley, burned some time before the Meadow Fire. You can see it's had more time to recover since the trail takes you through a veritable jungle of shoulder-high lupines, a typical fire-following species.

The canyon walls once again squeeze together as you climb out of the valley, passing below the dome of Bunnell Point across the river, above the spot where the water pours over the long, slippery slide of Bunnell Cascade. There aren't any good camping spots until you have gone another half mile or so, where you will find a fine backpackers campsite with log tables and chairs in an opening in the forest just past Lost Valley.

Just beyond the backpackers camp-site, two bridges take you back to the south side of the Merced River, where you begin a grueling climb partway up out of the gorge on shadeless switchbacks blasted out of the moun-tainside. As you pause to wipe away the sweat, you can marvel at one of Yosemite's most breathtaking, unpar-alleled, fabulously superior panoramas of the river pouring through the spec-tacular Merced Gorge. Toward the top of this climb, you pass in and out of a couple of buggy little forested spots with trickles of water nourishing tiny white orchids, and lots of mosquitoes.

After crossing back over to the north side of the river on another bridge, you meet the junction with the Sunrise Trail in Echo Valley at mile 10.5. Several creeks come together here and you must cross three more bridges before passing through several little meadows.

These orchids are pollinated by mosquitoes.

Now you begin the final stage of the finest section of this route, the grand (well, maybe the small) finale the river has been saving for last. This section of trail has also been carved out of the parent rock beside another exquisite, but smaller, more intimate rocky gorge. The scale of this one is perfect, with spots where you could dangle your toes in the water without being swept away. Here the stream descends in a series of small but extremely varied and interesting rapids, miniature waterfalls, deep holes, and swirling eddies for almost a mile before water emerges quietly from the forest that circles Merced Lake. A sign says "Merced Lake 7,250 feet," and other signs remind you that camping and fires are prohibited anywhere along the lakeshore. Skirt the north side of the lake for about a mile until you spot the rock paths leading to the right toward the tent cabins of Merced Lake High Sierra Camp at mile 13.1.

The backpackers campsite is right next door. Those who are not guests of the camp are welcome to use the spigot with potable water there and buy snacks when

▶ **Did you know that only female mosquitoes bite? They need the protein in your blood to make baby mosquitoes. The males, on the other hand, flit from flower to flower sipping nectar, and mating, of course, with females. Botanists say mosquitoes are the pollinators of the little white Sierra rein orchids.**

This is a classic Merced waterwheel.

the "store" (consisting of a few candy bars, maps, and mosquito repellent) is open, but they are requested to use the toilets in the backpackers area, and . . . wonder of wonders . . . they actually flush!

From here you can return to Yosemite Valley, head north toward Vogelsang High Sierra Camp on either the Fletcher Creek or Lewis Creek Trail, continue south along the Merced, passing pretty Washburn Lake and climbing over Red Peak Pass, or leave Yosemite and enter the Ansel Adams Wilderness at Isberg Pass.

Miles and Directions

0.0   Happy Isles
0.8   Vernal Fall Bridge
0.9   Turn right onto the John Muir Trail
2.3   Clark Point; keep right again on the John Muir Trail
3.3   Panorama Trail junction; keep left toward Nevada Fall
3.5   Cross the bridge over Nevada Fall
3.8   Mist Trail joins this one at a restroom; keep right
4.3   Keep straight ahead as the trail to Half Dome goes left
4.8   Little Yosemite Valley
6.8   Merced River Falls
7.9   Bunnell Cascade
10.5   Echo Valley; turn right toward Merced Lake
13.1   Merced Lake High Sierra Camp
26.2   Arrive back at the trailhead

◄   *Yet another Merced River cascade*

31 Fletcher Creek Cascades

One of the most exciting, dramatic (and most photographed) section of trail on the High Sierra Camp loop lies between Merced Lake and Vogelsang High Sierra Camps. You will have to make a serious climb from Merced Lake, or an equally serious descent from Vogelsang, but the rewards are great. Shining, usually rushing, Fletcher Creek takes on every form of falling water you ever imagined, from scenic cascades to powerful waterslides racing hundreds of feet through smooth rock chutes beneath classic granite domes. All this excitement alternates with sections of easy hiking beside meandering streams through green meadows. The trail is constructed so that much of the most interesting sections of the creek are visible from the trail, not hidden away in deep forest. Fletcher Creek flows for most of the summer too, though, of course, the grandest show takes place in early season. You can also make side trips to Emeric and Babcock Lakes, where there is some camping.

Height of fall: Indeterminate
Start: Happy Isles
Distance: 37.4 miles out and back
Hiking time: 3–5 days
Elevation change: 9,600 feet
Difficulty: Strenuous
Season: Late June through Aug

Nearest facilities: Everything you need but gas in Yosemite Valley and Tuolumne Meadows. Snacks, water, toilets at Merced Lake HSC.
Permits: Available in advance or from the wilderness center at Yosemite Village
Maps: Half Dome, Merced Peak, Vogelsang Peak

Finding the trailhead: Take the free shuttle bus to Happy Isles (stop 16) or park in the hikers' lot east of Curry (Half Dome) Village, turn right (east) at the far end of the lot, and follow the well-marked path to Happy Isles. This will add a mile round-trip to your hike. Continue on the paved road over the Happy Isles Bridge, then turn right (south), following the river upstream to the big sign on the left that marks the beginning of the John Muir Trail. Trailhead GPS: N37 43.51' / W119 33.33'

The Hike

Leave the wide path that runs southward along the Merced and turn left up the narrower trail into the forest, where in a few feet you will find a big sign marking the beginning of the John Muir Trail, with mileages listed all the way to Mount Whitney. The route climbs through black oak and pine forest among enormous lichen-draped boulders along the southeast bank of the Merced. A little spring trickles out of the rocks a few hundred yards up on your left. (**Note:** Don't drink the water here without purifying it.) After about 0.4 mile look across the Merced to your right. Tucked into Illilouette Gorge, Illilouette Fall pours 370 feet down the Panorama Cliff to meet the Merced River. It's a big, beautiful waterfall, but most people miss it. The trail makes a

Fletcher Creek slide MARTA KIS

short descent to a bridge at 0.8 mile, where dozens of visitors will be taking photos of 317-foot Vernal Fall upstream. There are restrooms, a water fountain, and dozens of freeloading ground squirrels near the bridge. For their health and your safety, do not feed them.

Cross the bridge to the south side of the river and turn left, upstream. At 1.1 mile the Mist Trail continues straight head. Keep right on the John Muir Trail and ascend on well-graded switchbacks through mixed conifer forest until you round a corner to Clark Point at mile 2.1, where one of the most spectacular of Yosemite's many overlooks will stop you in your tracks. Nevada Fall thunders down the canyon straight ahead in classic postcard style. The rounded shape behind and just to the left of Liberty Cap and Mount Broderick, which are just to the left of the fall, is the back side of Half Dome.

From Clark Point turn right, climb a few more switchbacks, then pass through a cut in the side of the cliff beneath a weeping rock overhang that drizzles water onto the trail and onto delicate ferns, columbines, and tiny white orchids. Now you lose a little elevation, and at mile 3.1 pass through an open gate at a junction with the Panorama Trail. Continue left through a shady little gully where water sometimes pools deeply enough to slosh over the tops of your boots, then round a corner to emerge onto a sunny bench and cross the bridge over the river. Just beyond, Nevada Fall crashes through an impossibly narrow notch and is visible all the way to the bottom, sometimes projecting a rainbow near the base. Stay behind protective railings

Fletcher Creek Cascades

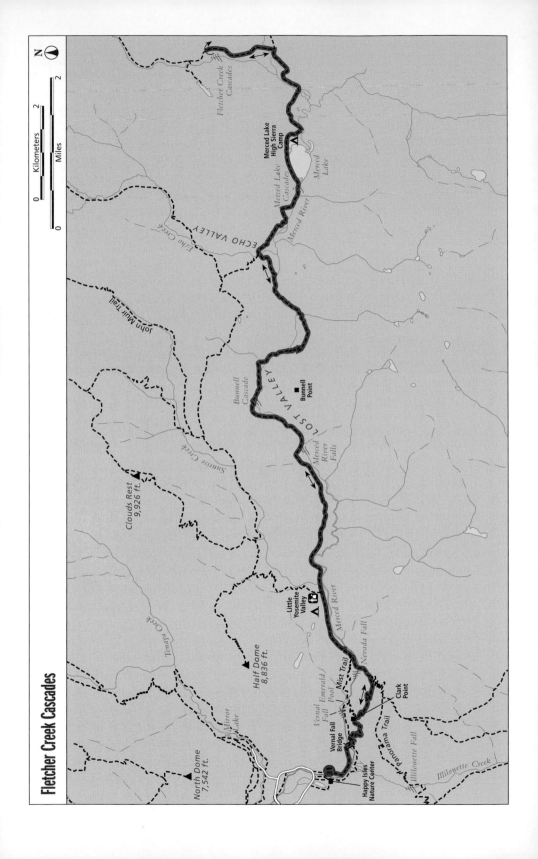

Fletcher Creek Cascades

Merced Lake
High Sierra Camp

Merced Lake
Cascades

ECHO VALLEY

Echo Creek

Merced River

Merced Lake

John Muir Trail

Bunnell
Cascade

LOST VALLEY

Bunnell
Point

Merced River
Falls

Sunrise Creek

Clouds Rest
9,926 ft.

Little
Yosemite
Valley

Half Dome
8,836 ft.

Tenaya Creek

Mirror
Lake

North Dome
7,542 ft.

Merced River

Mist Trail

Emerald
Pool

Vernal
Fall

Nevada Fall

Clark Point

Panorama Trail

Vernal Fall
Bridge

Happy Isles
Nature Center

Illilouette Fall

Illilouette Creek

N

Kilometers
0   2

Miles
0   2

and heed the warnings about wading or swimming above the falls. There have been fatalities here.

From the north side of the river, climb to a junction with the upper end of the Mist Trail. Continue upstream, climbing the well-defined trail over inlaid rocks. The way soon levels out and passes from sunlight into shade, and the Merced changes from a rushing, raging torrent to become quiet, dark, and deep. At 4.3 miles your trail parts company with the John Muir Trail, which heads off to the left (northeast) toward Half Dome while you continue straight ahead to Little Yosemite Valley, your first camping opportunity, at mile 4.8. It's a busy and popular place, especially for bears. There is also an architecturally elegant two-story solar composting toilet to admire, and two communal fire rings for campers to share. Please do not scar this already overused area by building another one.

Camping is prohibited for 2 more miles beyond the campground to the end of Little Yosemite Valley. It is not an inviting place to camp anyway, since the 2014 Meadow Fire has reduced it to a shadeless collection of black stumps.

At mile 6.8 the cliff walls pinch together beneath Moraine Dome, forcing the Merced, which has been out of sight for the last mile or so, into a gushing, glorious cascade tumbling down into the devastated valley. Above this first cascade the Merced slows and widens out once again through Lost Valley, burned sometime before the Meadow Fire. It's had more time to recover since the trail passes through a jungle of shoulder-high lupines, typical fire followers.

The canyon walls once again squeeze together as you climb out of the valley below the dome of Bunnell Point, below which the water pours over the long, slippery slide of Bunnell Cascade. There aren't any good camping spots until you have gone another half mile or so where there is a fine backpackers campsite with log tables and chairs in an opening in the forest just past Lost Valley.

Just beyond the backpackers campsite, two bridges take you back to the south side of the Merced River, where you begin a grueling climb partway up out of the gorge on shadeless switchbacks blasted out of the mountainside. As you pause to wipe away the sweat, you can marvel at one of Yosemite's most breathtaking panoramas of the river pouring through the spectacular Merced Gorge. Toward the top of this climb, you pass in and out of a couple of buggy little forested spots with trickles of water nourishing tiny white orchids and lots of mosquitoes.

After crossing back over to the north side of the river on another bridge, you meet the junction with the Sunrise Trail in Echo Valley at mile 10.5. Several creeks come together here and you must cross three more bridges before passing through several little meadows.

The next section of trail, the last before you reach Merced Lake, has also been carved out of the parent rock beside another gorge, something like the last one, but this one is smaller and more exquisitely proportioned than the one below. You could dangle your toes in the water here without being swept away as the stream descends in a series of small but extremely varied and interesting rapids, miniature waterfalls,

Fletcher Creek flows down a pretty cascade. STEVEN BAKOS

cascades, deep holes, little waterwheels, and swirling eddies for almost a mile until you arrive at Merced Lake, where a sign (only slightly incorrect) says you are at 7,250 feet.

Skirt the north side of the lake for about a mile until you spot the rock paths leading to the right toward the tent cabins of Merced Lake High Sierra Camp at mile 13.1. The backpackers campsite is right next door. Those who are not guests of the camp are welcome to use the spigot with potable water there and buy snacks from the "store" when it's open, but are requested to use the (flush!) toilets in the backpackers area.

Now on your way to Vogelsang, walk east through lodgepole pine and fir forest, crossing several little creeks on footbridges. At 13.3 miles the Merced Lake Ranger Station and corral appear on the right. Turn left (north) at the junction here and switchback steeply up above Lewis Creek to meet the Fletcher Creek Trail at 16.2 miles. From here you can catch good views up the Fletcher Creek drainage and back down to Merced Lake and all the way to Half Dome in the far distance if the sky is clear. You have two choices of routes to Vogelsang from this junction. The Lewis Creek Trail climbs up over 10,700-foot Vogelsang Pass and is wildly scenic, but waterfall lovers should take the left (western) Fletcher Creek Trail at mile 16.7. Cross Fletcher Creek on a bridge and begin to climb relentless switchbacks on sometimes open rocky trail with more great views. There are some beautiful cascades along the trail. Climb up above the creek in some forest with views of a pretty cascade beyond which, on the other side of the creek, is a distinctive but oddly unnamed dome.

Descend a bit to meet the Babcock Lake turnoff at mile 17.6, then enjoy a little reprieve from climbing (or descending) through forest, before climbing again alongside one of the longest, steepest, most exciting waterslides ever. Once you have passed the spot where Emeric Creek joins Fletcher Creek, you enter a restful section of trail beside a beautiful meadow along a meandering creek, which you eventually rock-hop across. Continue on to the Emeric Lake turnoff at 18.7 miles. Just beyond, the trail splits. Keep right (east) and rejoin Fletcher Creek for a time, then continuing north, climb moderately to Vogelsang High Sierra Camp at mile 19.9.

If you have arranged a shuttle, you can head down the Rafferty Creek Trail for 6.7 more miles to Tuolumne Meadows. You can also return the way you came, or you can make a grand loop, climbing Vogelsang Pass, returning to Merced Lake via Lewis Creek or any number of loop trip options.

Miles and Directions

0.0 Happy Isles

0.8 Vernal Fall Bridge

0.9 Turn right onto the John Muir Trail

2.3 Clark Point; keep right again on the John Muir Trail

3.3 Panorama Trail junction; keep left toward Nevada Fall

3.5 Cross the bridge over Nevada Fall

3.8 Mist Trail joins this one at a restroom; keep right

4.3 Keep straight ahead as the trail to Half Dome goes left

4.8 Little Yosemite Valley Camp

6.8 Merced River Falls

7.9 Bunnell Cascade

10.5 Echo Valley; turn right toward Merced Lake

13.1 Merced Lake High Sierra Camp

13.3 Merced Lake Ranger Station

16.7 Fletcher Creek Trail; keep left

17.6 Babcock Lake turnoff

18.7 Fletcher Creek Cascade

37.4 Arrive back at Happy Isles

OR

19.9 Continue on to Vogelsang High Sierra Camp

26.6 Arrive at Tuolumne Meadows and return to Yosemite Valley via Tioga Road

Option: If you just want to see fabulous Fletcher Creek alone, the most direct route starts from Tuolumne Meadows and climbs via Rafferty Creek to Vogelsang. From the junction just south of the High Sierra Camp, follow the right (southwest) fork toward Emeric and/or Babcock Lakes.

32 Vogelsang Cascades

Vogelsang is the highest of the camps on the High Sierra Camp loop, at 10,130 feet, so whether you approach it from Merced Lake Camp as part of the loop or choose the shortest distance from a road, there are cascades (not major named ones but beauties just the same) running right through the camp or very nearby.

The big peak immediately behind the camp is Fletcher Peak, and the lake beneath it is Fletcher Lake, not Vogelsang Lake as you might expect. You can head around the north side of Fletcher Lake to find a little waterfall connecting Fletcher Lake to Townsley Lake, the one above it. There is no official trail between these two lakes, but it's an easy and enjoyable scramble following the little waterfalls to the top. The wildflowers among the rocks of this little connecting stream are especially fine.

Height of falls: Various
Start: Dog Lake parking lot / John Muir Trailhead
Distance: 14.0 miles out and back
Hiking time: Most of the day, or spend the night
Elevation change: 4,060 feet
Difficulty: Moderate

Nearest facilities: Emergency supplies, toilets at the High Sierra Camp. Emergency supplies, snacks at Vogelsang "store."
Permits: None for a day hike. Available in advance or from the wilderness center at Yosemite Village.
Maps: USGS Vogelsang Peak

Finding the trailhead: From the west, drive Tioga Road (CA 120) eastward past the Tuolumne Meadows Visitor Center, store, and campground, all on the right. Cross the bridge over the Tuolumne River. In about a mile, turn right at the entrance to the wilderness center, and follow the road as it curves to the left for about 0.5 mile to the Dog Lake parking lot on the left. The trailhead is on the right (south) side of the road. Trailhead GPS: N37 52.39' / W119 20.20'

The Hike

Cross the road south of the parking lot to the "John Muir Trailhead" sign. Follow the John Muir Trail southeast to a footbridge over the Dana Fork of the Tuolumne River at 0.2 mile. Ignore the cutoff back to the Tuolumne Meadows Lodge, cross the bridge, then turn left and follow the river upstream, pausing to enjoy wildflower gardens along the shore where dozens of different species vie for attention. The route now bends slightly to the right, crosses a low rise alongside a marshy area, and reaches the twin bridges over the Lyell Fork of the Tuolumne at 0.6 mile. This is surely one of the most sublime (and most photographed) vistas in Yosemite, with the clear turquoise-water river winding toward you through the green meadow. At your feet deep bowls have been worn into the granite by the scouring force of silt carried from the mountains by spring runoff, and the water swirls in beautiful patterns from one bowl to the next. The massive gray bulk on your left is Mammoth Peak (not to be confused with Mammoth Mountain, the ski resort that lies farther south).

Soon after you leave the twin bridges, ignore another path that leads back (right) to the Tuolumne Meadows Campground at mile 0.7. Hike easily through lodgepole forest to mile 1.5, where you leave the John Muir Trail as it heads left (east) and crosses another bridge. You keep to the right and begin to climb, quite steeply at first, until the grade becomes easier, usually under shady forest cover, alternating with small sunny openings. You will be crossing a couple of creeks flowing down from the right that sometimes require just a quick skip across, sometimes a more serious rock hop, or even wading at high water.

In another mile you will begin to hear Rafferty Creek rushing over rocks to your left.

Vogelsang Peak just below Vogelsang Pass offers great views.

Most of the time it's out of sight, but on two or three occasions, the trail comes close enough to the creek side to get a glimpse. Once you have reached mile 3.0 and have crossed over two side streams and have come close enough to the creek to catch sight of it twice, keep an eye out for a spot where the forest becomes more sparse and rocky and you pass a prominent granite ridge on your right with three "bumps." These bumps aren't named on the topo, but the nearest one to you is marked 9801. (If you have your GPS with you, the coordinates are N37 50.57' / W119 19.20'.) On your left Rafferty Creek, which has been flowing north, suddenly makes a sharp

▶ Whenever you see parallel paths all but one of which have tree branches and other small obstacles strewn along them, trail builders are asking you to walk on the unblocked path only, in order to allow the other scars to heal and to prevent the route from looking like a four- (or more) lane highway.

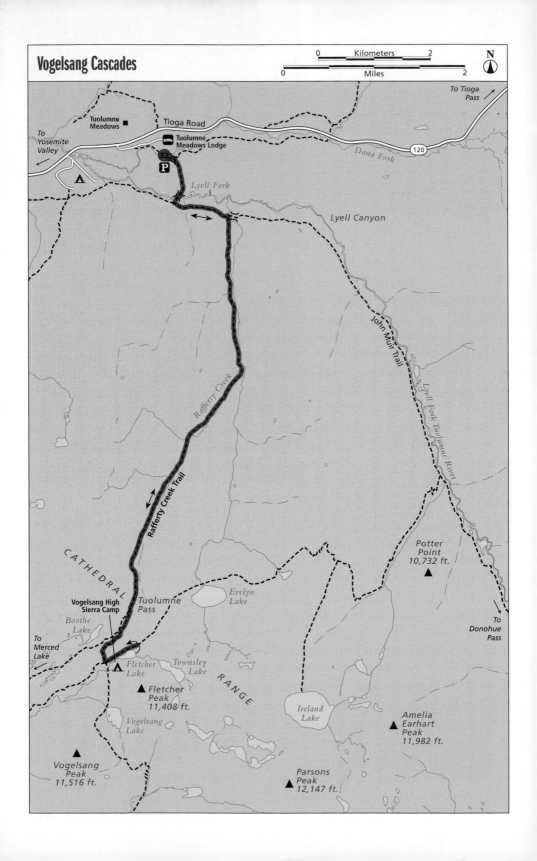

Vogelsang Cascades

0 Kilometers 2

0 Miles 2

N

To Tioga Pass

To Yosemite Valley

Tuolumne Meadows

Tioga Road

Tuolumne Meadows Lodge

P

120

Dana Fork

Lyell Fork

Lyell Canyon

Lyell Fork Tuolumne River

John Muir Trail

Rafferty Creek

Rafferty Creek Trail

CATHEDRAL

Evelyn Lake

Potter Point 10,732 ft.

Vogelsang High Sierra Camp

Tuolumne Pass

Boothe Lake

To Merced Lake

Fletcher Lake

Townsley Lake

RANGE

Ireland Lake

To Donohue Pass

Fletcher Peak 11,408 ft.

Vogelsang Lake

Amelia Earhart Peak 11,982 ft.

Vogelsang Peak 11,516 ft.

Parsons Peak 12,147 ft.

turn toward you and drops over a long low ridge in two places to form double Rafferty Creek Falls, before resuming its southward course. This is a delightful rest or lunch stop early in the season where two pretty little cascades flow side by side, each creating its own sandy-bottomed pool just perfect for you, or a couple, or a family, to splash in. It's down in a little gully, so you will have to watch for it. Continue on your way upward. The Rafferty Creek Trail has been rerouted away from its former path close alongside Rafferty Creek, where too many footprints and horseshoes

These tiny squirrels, also known as picket pins, populate high meadows.

have worn parallel deep ruts in the fragile meadow. The trail now runs higher above the creek along more resistant rocks, which helps prevent erosion but takes you farther away from the stream.

After a half mile of steeper climbing in shade, the way becomes much more open as you approach tree line, and the river gurgles quietly nearby. This open section of trail is awkward to hike. It was lined with big rocks to keep hikers on the main path, but the main path has now become worn into its own ruts, forcing you to hop from rock to rock or to make giant steps every few feet that are exhausting. At mile 5.6 you reach the top of not-very-dramatic Tuolumne Pass, where you find a junction. Boothe Lake and Fletcher Creek Trail continue on over the pass. A trail sign says it's 0.8 mile to Vogelsang. After one last shady and flower-lined climb heading temporarily back north, you emerge into the big open meadow before Vogelsang High Sierra Camp with its cluster of tent cabins and stone headquarters, kitchen, and "store."

You can buy snacks and some emergency items, but the tap water at the camp is not potable, and the toilets are for guests only, so overnight backpackers are routed to a beautiful area to the north of the camp overlooking the Rafferty Creek drainage with gorgeous views of Mount Conness and the peaks on the northern border of the park. Vogelsang occupies one of the most scenic sites in all of Yosemite, with Fletcher Peak as its backdrop and Fletcher Lake at its base. If, when you first arrive, you head toward the main entrance marked "Vogelsang High Sierra Camp 10,130 feet," you meet a delightful and complex series of cascades pouring out of Fletcher Lake just beyond. Until August Fletcher Creek runs high enough that you'll have to seek out a safe place downstream to cross.

This is the prettiest stream around, but you're likely not to pay as much attention to it as it deserves since it's in the middle of all the High Sierra Camp activity. If you would like a more private, or at least a more quiet, cascade to contemplate, walk through the meadow passing the cluster of tent cabins on the right, then passing the

Several little waterfalls feed Fletcher Lake at Vogelsang.

backpackers' area on the left, and follow the shore of Fletcher Lake toward its inlet. Another cascade follows interesting patterns over and through pretty rock gardens as it descends, from Townsley Lake, just above. You can follow the path of this stream fairly easily to the upper lake, which has a wilder, more definite alpine character. It's another beautiful lake to explore, and above it is yet another, smaller lake called Hanging Basket that may contribute its own cascade.

From here you can return to Tuolumne Meadows the way you came, or return via the longer Lyell Fork route (11.5 miles). (This lower section of the route is part of the John Muir Trail, so there will be more traffic). Or you can continue up over Vogelsang Pass at 10,700 feet or over Tuolumne Pass at 10,000 feet, and continue on down to the next High Sierra Camp at Merced Lake.

Miles and Directions

0.0 Dog Lake parking lot / John Muir Trailhead
0.2 Junction with Tuolumne Meadows Lodge; keep right
0.3 Gaylor Lakes Trail; keep right
0.6 Cross the twin bridges over the Lyell Fork; turn left
1.3 Rafferty Creek Trail junction; keep right
5.6 Tuolumne Pass / Boothe Lake junction
6.7 Vogelsang High Sierra Camp
14.0 Arrive back at the trailhead

Waterfalls of the Tuolumne Meadows Region

Tuolumne Meadows is the largest meadow complex in Yosemite and one of the largest in the Sierra Nevada range. The Lyell Fork of the Tuolumne River originates at the Lyell Glacier on Mount Lyell, and the Dana Fork arises from snowfields on the southern slope of Mount Dana. The two forks meet here at about 8,600 feet, mingle, and wander in beautiful wide curves northwest for a few miles, before they begin their headlong rush down the Grand Canyon of the Tuolumne. Its waters are collected in Hetch Hetchy Reservoir, where they are tamed by several dams and join the San Joaquin River to serve the San Francisco region.

Just east of Tuolumne, Dana Meadows is another door to the backcountry.

Tuolumne Meadows, the eastern center of activity in Yosemite, is accessible only in summer.

It's a vast glacial landscape with classic glacial features like erratic boulders, glacial striations and polish, roches moutonnées, and silted-in glacial tarns. Unlike the glaciers that shaped Yosemite Valley, the ice here simply spread out over broad and open meadows, so cliffs for waterfalls to pour over are farther apart, but there are some real beauties here.

Tuolumne Meadows is a bustling place, the second-most populous area in Yosemite, a veritable village with a (tented) lodge, store, restaurant, post office, visitor center, and campground, though these amenities are dismantled in winter when the Tioga Pass is closed.

Most of the waterfalls in this section can be reached via day hikes, though many involve a full day's effort and a few require a relatively short overnight backpack. The competition for wilderness permits is intense because the season is short. The meadows get an average of 6 to 8 feet of snow with much variation from year to year, so you can't get started until the Tioga Road is open, sometimes in early June, sometimes not until July. It closes again with the first major snowfall, occasionally as early as October. So, the season is short, the landscape spectacular, big population centers like San Francisco and Los Angeles are relatively close by, and once you're there, you're already at high elevation. In addition, it is a rest and resupply stop on both the John Muir and Pacific Crest Trails, so special wilderness permit rules apply for overnight hikes.

33 Rafferty Creek Falls

Rafferty Creek is one of the two primary routes between Tuolumne Meadows and Vogelsang High Sierra Camp. Rafferty is the shortest route to Vogelsang, but the other route, the Lyell Fork, is part of the John Muir Trail and gets more traffic.

These little falls aren't marked in any way, so you will have to pay close attention to the directions and hope for a little luck. Sometimes the squeals of delight from people who have discovered the spot will guide you there. On the other hand, once you have found it, you might just be lucky enough to have it to yourself since it's a bit off the trail. Fortunately, it is not far enough along the path away from the nearest road to be legal for overnight camping, or it would be overrun in no time.

These are almost identical twin waterfalls—not very big—that seem to be proportioned just for humans. Here, Rafferty Creek flows south to north, then makes a sudden almost-right-angle turn to the east, where it drops into a little gorge perhaps 20 feet deep, then abruptly turns north again. Two main notches of about equal size release water of fairly equal volume into the gorge where the stream changes direction. The two falls flow about 40 feet apart onto the sandy bottom of the gorge, creating individual shallow his/hers, hers/hers, his/his pools, though very early in spring there is enough flow for the pools to coalesce. It's a short, easy scramble to get into the gorge.

Height of falls: 20 feet
Start: Dog Lake parking lot / John Muir Trailhead
Distance: 7.4 miles out and back
Hiking time: 3–4 hours
Elevation change: 800 feet
Difficulty: Easy
Seasons: Spring, summer, whenever Tioga Road is open
Nearest facilities: Food, water, phones at Tuolumne Meadows Village; gas at Lee Vining

Permits: None
Maps: Vogelsang Peak
Special considerations: There aren't many obvious clear waypoints or markers to help you find these falls, and neither the USGS topo nor the commercial maps are perfectly accurate since the trail has been slightly rerouted over the years. But none of these changes affect this hike and the topo may be useful though not essential.

Finding the trailhead: From the west drive Tioga Road (CA 120) eastward past the Tuolumne Meadows Visitor Center, store, and campground, all on the right. Cross the bridge over the Tuolumne River. After about a mile turn right at the entrance to the wilderness center. Follow the road as it curves around to the left for about a half mile to the Dog Lake parking lot on the left. Leave ice chests and all food in the bear-proof boxes. From Tioga Pass follow the Tioga Road west past the turnoff to the wilderness center and the Tuolumne Lodge on the left, and follow the road to the Dog Lake parking lot, also on the left. Trailhead GPS: N37 52.39' / W119 20.20'

You can each have your own personal pool at Rafferty Creek.

The Hike

Cross the road south of the parking lot to the "John Muir Trailhead" sign. Follow the trail southeast to the footbridge over the Dana Fork at 0.2 mile. Ignore the cutoff back to the lodge and cross the bridge, then turn left and follow the river upstream. The route bends slightly to the right, crosses a low rise, and reaches the twin bridges over the Lyell Fork at 0.6 mile. Here you will find one of the premier and most photographed views in the Tuolumne area, where the turquoise water traces sensuous patterns as it flows over the rounded rocks. In just a few yards, ignore a trail that turns off to the right back toward the Tuolumne Meadows Campground. Hike easily through lodgepole forest to mile 1.5 where you leave the John Muir Trail as it heads left (east) and crosses another bridge. You keep to the right and begin to climb sometimes steeply, sometimes less so, usually under shady forest cover, alternating with small sunny openings. You will be crossing a couple of creeks flowing down from the right, sometimes just a quick skip across, a rock hop, or even wading at high water.

In about another mile you will begin to hear Rafferty Creek rushing over rocks to your left. Most of the time it's out of sight, but on two or three occasions, the trail comes close enough to the creek side to get a glimpse. After you have reached mile 3.0, have crossed over two side streams, and have come close enough to the creek to catch sight of it twice, start looking for your goal. To the right the forest becomes sparser,

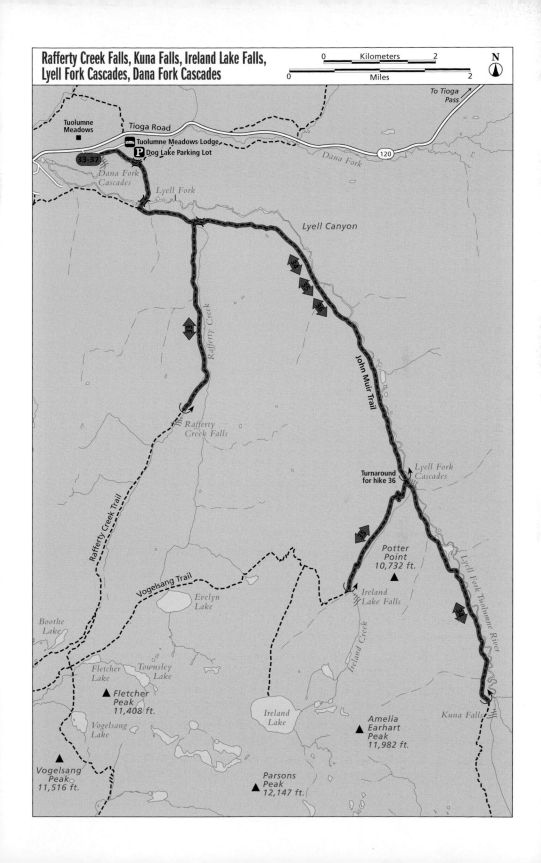

Rafferty Creek Falls, Kuna Falls, Ireland Lake Falls, Lyell Fork Cascades, Dana Fork Cascades

Kilometers
0   2

Miles
0   2

N

To Tioga Pass

Tuolumne Meadows

Tioga Road

Tuolumne Meadows Lodge

Dog Lake Parking Lot

120

Dana Fork

33-37

Dana Fork Cascades

Lyell Fork

Lyell Canyon

34

35

36

33

Rafferty Creek

Rafferty Creek Falls

John Muir Trail

Lyell Fork Cascades

Turnaround for hike 36

Rafferty Creek Trail

Vogelsang Trail

Potter Point 10,732 ft.

35

Evelyn Lake

Ireland Lake Falls

Lyell Fork Tuolumne River

Boothe Lake

Ireland Creek

Fletcher Lake

Townsley Lake

Fletcher Peak 11,408 ft.

Ireland Lake

Vogelsang Lake

Amelia Earhart Peak 11,982 ft.

Kuna Falls

Vogelsang Peak 11,516 ft.

Parsons Peak 12,147 ft.

These little falls run only into July.

and you pass a prominent bare granite ridge with three "bumps." The bump farthest right is the biggest one, the smaller two are closer to you. As you proceed, the biggest and farthest bump disappears, then the middle one slowly vanishes, and the one near-est the trail seems to point right at you. (These bumps aren't named on the topo, but the nearest one to you and your goal is marked 9801.) As soon as you pass this point and are looking at the ridge from the side, stay alert. Rafferty Creek Falls are near. On a warm and busy day, you may hear other hikers enjoying the pools. This is where Rafferty Creek, which has been flowing north, suddenly makes a sharp turn to the left, drops over a long, low ridge forming double Rafferty Falls, then abruptly resumes

These little falls and pools make refreshing rest stops.

its northward course. There are a couple of pretty little cascades both upstream and downstream of the main falls and pools as well. The GPS is N37 50.34' / W119 19.15'.

Miles and Directions

0.0 Dog Lake parking lot / John Muir Trailhead

0.2 Bridge over Dana Fork; keep right

0.3 Gaylor Lakes Trail; keep right

0.7 Cutoff to Tuolumne Meadows Campground; turn left

1.3 Rafferty Creek Trail junction; keep right

3.7 Rafferty Falls

7.4 Arrive back at the trailhead

34 Kuna Falls

A long cascade fed by little lakes high up on the Kuna Crest makes a long, shimmering descent to the Lyell Fork of the Tuolumne River. It separates into a number of streamers, some of these separating again into lacy patterns before vanishing into the forest. It is such a tall waterfall/cascade combination that it's hard to include in a single photograph—it's probably most interesting as a video. It is easily visible from the John Muir Trail, which follows the river through the Lyell Fork Canyon on its way up to Mount Lyell, the tallest peak in Yosemite, which shelters Yosemite's largest glacier. The cascade/fall is on the opposite side of the river from the trail, and you will probably want to get closer to it, but your best view is from the trail. The closer you get to the fall, the less of it you can see. There is a good campsite not far off the trail, and the best time to see it is in the afternoon.

Height of falls: About 1,200 feet
Start: Dog Lake parking lot / John Muir Trailhead
Distance: 16.0 miles out and back
Hiking time: 10-12 hours or overnight
Elevation change: 600 feet
Difficulty: Strenuous as a day hike, easy to moderate as a backpack
Seasons: July–Sept, but the earlier the season, the most impressive the falls; after the Tioga Road is open

Nearest facilities: Groceries, cafe, phones at Tuolumne Meadows; gas at Lee Vining and Crane Flat
Permits: None for a day hike; available in advance or from the Tuolumne Meadows Wilderness Center
Maps: Tioga Pass and Vogelsang Peak quads
Special considerations: This is a popular spot with bears. If you are backpacking, keep your bear canister locked.

Finding the trailhead: From the west drive Tioga Road (CA 120) eastward past the Tuolumne Meadows Visitor Center, store, and campground, all on the right. Cross the bridge over the Tuolumne River. In about a mile turn right at the entrance to the wilderness center. Follow the road as it curves to the left for about 0.5 mile to the Dog Lake parking lot on the left. The trailhead is on the right (south) side of the road. Trailhead GPS: N37 52.39' / W119 20.20'

The Hike

Cross the road south of the parking lot to the trailhead sign. Follow the John Muir Trail southeast to a footbridge over the Dana Fork at 0.2 mile. Ignore the cutoff back to the Tuolumne Meadows Lodge and cross the bridge, then turn left and follow the river upstream, pausing to enjoy wildflower gardens along the shore, where dozens of different species vie for attention. The route now bends slightly to the right, crosses a low rise alongside a marshy area, and reaches the twin bridges over the Lyell Fork at 0.6 mile. This is surely one of the most sublime vistas in Yosemite, with the clear turquoise river winding toward you through the green meadow. At your feet deep bowls have been worn into the granite by the scouring force of silt carried from the mountains by spring run-off, and the water swirls in beautiful patterns from one bowl to the next. The massive gray bulk on your left is Mammoth Peak (not to be confused with Mammoth Mountain, the ski resort, which lies farther south).

Soon after you leave the twin bridges, another path leads back (right) to the Tuolumne Meadows Campground at mile 0.7. Continue left on the John Muir Trail through lodgepole pine forest and over open rock to 1.3 miles, where the Rafferty Creek Trail heads uphill to the right. Cross the bridge over the creek on your left and continue through forest and meadows that in early season are a solid mass of pale-lavender shooting stars (and mosquitoes). Soon the sound of the river becomes apparent—it's been hidden for a while behind a low

Kuna Falls separates into many strands as it flows.

ridge—and a glorious view of Lyell Canyon opens up before you. Sometimes the river flows deep and clear; sometimes it slides over slickrock into perfect bathing pools. Any one of a thousand spots along the bank invites lunch, a snack, a sunbath, or a nap.

At 5.6 miles the John Muir Trail and the Vogelsang / Ireland Lake Trails split. Good campsites are just uphill to the right of the trail sign. Keep left at this junction and accompany the meandering river upstream through the meadow. A short distance after you make the turn where the sign just says "John Muir Trail," you'll have to make a rock or log crossing of Ireland Creek that can be challenging early in the year. The trail along the Lyell Fork has been reworked, moved higher up the side of the hill to protect the fragile meadow closer to the stream. In a couple of miles, you'll be able to spot the upper part of the falls on the other side of the canyon. It becomes louder and louder, and just beyond the point where the trail begins its climb up toward Donohue Pass, Kuna Creek drops down from the Kuna Crest to join the Tuolumne. There is a good view of the tall cascade right from the trail. If you are backpacking, there is a campsite nearby. If you are only out for the day, retrace your steps to the trailhead.

The height of Kuna Falls is impossible to measure.

Miles and Directions

0.0 John Muir Trailhead at Dog Lake parking lot

0.2 Footbridge over Dana Fork; cross bridge and turn left

0.3 Cutoff to Gaylor Lakes; keep right

0.6 Twin bridges

0.7 Tuolumne Meadows Campground cutoff; turn left

1.3 Rafferty Creek Trail junction; turn left, crossing the bridge

5.6 Vogelsang Trail junction; keep left

8.0 View of Kuna Falls from the trail

16.0 Arrive back at the trailhead

35 Ireland Lake Falls

After a mile of puffing your way up through forest for more than a mile, a lovely meadow with wildflowers appears in front of you, and at its upper end, a silvery cascade glides down from a hidden lake. It's a perfect snack or picnic stop on your way to Vogelsang High Sierra Camp or as an end in itself.

Height of falls: Indeterminate
Start: Dog Lake parking lot / John Muir Trailhead
Distance: 14.2 miles out and back
Hiking time: 6–8 hours or overnight
Elevation change: 2,000 feet
Difficulty: Moderate

Seasons: Late spring to early fall, whenever the Tioga Road is open
Nearest facilities: Tuolumne Meadows village
Permits: None for a day hike. Available in advance from the Tuolumne Meadows Wilderness Center for overnights.
Maps: USGS Vogelsang quad

Finding the trailhead: From the west drive Tioga Road (CA 120) eastward past the Tuolumne Meadows Visitor Center, store, and campground, all on the right. Cross the bridge over the Tuolumne River. In about a mile turn right at the entrance to the wilderness center. Follow the road as it curves to the left for about 0.5 mile to the Dog Lake parking lot on the left. The trailhead is on the right (south) side of the road. Trailhead GPS: N37 52.39' / W119 20.20'

While Ireland Lake itself is above timberline, it flows into deep forest.

A storm looms over Ireland Lake. STEVEN BAKOS

The Hike

Cross the road south of the parking lot to the trailhead sign. Follow the John Muir Trail southeast to a footbridge over the Dana Fork at 0.2 mile. Ignore the cutoff back to the Tuolumne Meadows Lodge and cross the bridge, then turn left and follow the river upstream, pausing to enjoy wildflower gardens along the shore, where dozens of different species vie for attention. The route now bends slightly to the right, crosses a low rise alongside a marshy area, and reaches the twin bridges over the Lyell Fork at 0.6 mile. This is surely one of the most sublime vistas in Yosemite, with the clear turquoise river winding toward you through the green meadow. At your feet deep bowls have been worn into the granite by the scouring force of silt carried from the mountains by spring runoff, and the water swirls in beautiful patterns from one bowl to the next. The massive gray bulk on your left is Mammoth Peak (not to be confused with Mammoth Mountain, the ski resort, which lies farther south).

Soon after you leave the twin bridges, another path leads back (right) to the Tuolumne Meadows Campground at mile 0.7. Continue left on the John Muir Trail through lodgepole pine forest and over open rock to 1.3 miles, where the Rafferty Creek Trail heads uphill to the right. Cross the bridge over the creek on your left and continue through forest and meadows that in early season are a solid mass of pale-lavender shooting stars (and mosquitoes). Soon the sound of the river becomes apparent—it's been hidden for a while behind a low ridge—and a glorious view of Lyell Canyon opens up before you. Sometimes the river flows deep and clear; sometimes it slides over slickrock into perfect bathing pools. Any one of a thousand spots along the bank invites lunch, a snack, a sunbath, or a nap.

At 5.6 miles the John Muir Trail and the Vogelsang / Ireland Lake Trails split. Good campsites are just uphill to the right of the trail sign. Continue climbing through forest until you see the little meadow with the waterfall at its head at 7.1 miles. It's flowing down from high, barren, but beautiful Ireland Lake. It might look like an ideal spot to camp, but there is really nowhere very close to the meadow that will keep you legal, that is, off vegetation, 100 feet from water, and 100 feet from the trail. If you must camp, hike a bit farther up into the forest, or return to the well-established campsite at the John Muir Trail / Vogelsang Trail junction 1.5 miles back. Return the way you came.

Miles and Directions

0.0   Dog Lake parking lot / John Muir Trailhead
0.2   Bridge over Dana Fork and junction with Tuolumne Meadows Lodge; keep right
0.3   Gaylor Lakes Trail; turn right
0.6   Cross the two bridges over the Lyell Fork
0.7   Cutoff to Tuolumne Meadows Campground
1.3   Rafferty Creek Trail junction; keep left and cross the bridge
5.6   John Muir Trail / Vogelsang Trail junction; turn right
7.1   Ireland Lake Falls
14.2   Arrive back at the trailhead

36 Lyell Fork Cascades

This is the first and the most beautiful set of significant cascades on the Tuolumne River as you head south along the open section of the Lyell Fork. They are far enough along the path for you to be ready for a rest or a dip on a hot day. They will draw your attention from the trail at any time of year by their music, but up until early July, no hiker can walk on past them without stopping for a while. There is a perfect configuration of smooth sliding rocks and miniature rooster tails and water-wheels to catch your eye, and they are deep enough in spring to early summer to exhibit that heavenly blue-green color that upstream glaciers produce by grinding solid rock into fine powder that reflects turquoise light.

Height of falls: Indeterminate
Start: Dog Lake parking lot / John Muir Trailhead
Distance: 10.6 miles out and back
Hiking time: 5-6 hours
Elevation change: 400 feet
Difficulty: Easy to moderate
Seasons: The Lyell Fork flows all year, but the falls are most spectacular May through early July.

Nearest facilities: Everything you need is in Tuolumne Village except gas. Nothing at the trailhead.
Permits: None for a day hike, available for overnights in advance or at the Tuolumne Meadows Wilderness Center
Maps: USGS Vogelsang Peak quad

Finding the trailhead: From the west drive Tioga Road (CA 120) eastward past the Tuolumne Meadows Visitor Center, store, and campground, all on the right. Cross the bridge over the Tuolumne River. In about a mile turn right at the entrance to the wilderness center. Follow the road as it curves to the left for about 0.5 mile to the Dog Lake parking lot on the left. The trail is on the right (south) side of the road. Trailhead GPS: N37 52.39' / W119 20.20'

The Hike

Cross the road south of the parking lot at the trailhead sign. Follow the John Muir Trail southeast to a footbridge over the Dana Fork of the Tuolumne at 0.2 mile. Ignore the cutoff back to the Tuolumne Meadows Lodge and cross the bridge, then turn left and follow the river upstream, pausing to enjoy wildflower gardens along the shore, where dozens of species vie for attention. The route now bends slightly to the right, crosses a low rise alongside a marshy area, and reaches the twin bridges over the Lyell Fork at 0.6 mile. This is surely one of the most sublime vistas in Yosemite, with the clear turquoise water winding toward you through the green meadow. At your feet deep bowls have been worn into the granite by the scouring force of silt carried from the mountains by spring runoff, and the water swirls in beautiful patterns from one

The Lyell Fork of the Tuolumne River offers opportunities for wading.

The Tuolumne River has many inviting pools and cascades.

▶ In the old days most popular campsites (like this one) were furnished with ugly "bear cables." Sturdy wire was strung between two poles where hikers were expected to hang their food bags out of the reach of bears. It required some very special techniques and a powerful throwing arm. Sometimes it worked, sometimes it didn't, but it did provide much hilarious after-dinner entertainment night after night. Bear canisters have ended all that. In fact, hanging your food from tree branches or anything else is now illegal in Yosemite.

bowl to the next. The massive gray bulk on your left is Mammoth Peak (not to be confused with Mammoth Mountain, the ski resort, which lies farther south).

Soon after you leave the twin bridges, another path leads back (right) to the Tuolumne Meadows Campground at mile 0.7. Continue left on the John Muir Trail through lodgepole pine forest alternating with open rock to a junction at 1.3 miles, where the Rafferty Creek Trail heads uphill to the right. Turn left and cross the bridge over the creek and continue through forest and meadows that in early season are a solid mass of pale-lavender shooting stars (and mosquitoes). Soon the sound of the river becomes apparent—it's been hidden for a while behind a low ridge—and a glorious view of Lyell Canyon opens up before you.

As soon as you reach this open spot, a use trail angles off toward the river for perhaps 50 yards to a spot with some pretty, but minor, cascades where many hikers before you have been unable to resist a rest break. Back on the trail, you gain elevation slightly, now and then within sight and sound of the Tuolumne, where the river swirls in beautiful patterns from one bowl to the next.

These cascades are very close to the trail, so when you see the river right beside you, watch the trail at your feet where there is a set of six neat stairsteps to help you

Lyell Cascades make tempting rest stops.

gain a little elevation. You should notice them because this trail seldom has such a regular pattern. There is a fairly long view downstream where the river makes some lovely curves, but the best is right in front of you, a couple of perfect pools shallow enough for sitting (safely) and deep enough to sink in up to your upper half. There are waterslides connecting them, little rooster tails where the stream hits a groove or is thrown into the air by a low rock barrier. They look as though they were designed on purpose for maximum aesthetic effect and enjoyment.

For backpackers especially, the first good camping spot along the Lyell Fork is found at the junction of the Vogelsang and John Muir Trails, about 5.6 miles in, 10 to 15 minutes beyond the cascade. It's a good short day's stopping place if you got a late start. This campsite isn't clearly visible from the trail so you have to look uphill just a few feet to the right as you are heading south. It has space for several tents and a well-used fire ring.

Miles and Directions

0.0 Dog Lake parking lot / John Muir Trailhead

0.2 Footbridge over Dana Fork; cross the bridge and turn left

0.3 Cutoff to Gaylor Lakes; keep right

0.6 Twin bridges

0.7 Tuolumne Meadows Campground cutoff; keep left

1.3 Rafferty Creek Trail junction; turn left, crossing the bridge

5.3 Best Lyell Fork Cascades

10.6 Arrive back at the trailhead

37 Dana Fork Cascades

This short section of the Dana Fork of the Tuolumne River is within minutes of a major trailhead and just a few steps off the John Muir Trail, but most hikers seem to miss it. There are usually a few anglers, picnickers, and sunbathers, but this spot never seems to draw the crowds it deserves, partly because it's halfway hidden.

The rock of the streambed has been carved and smoothed in such intricate curves and hollows, such perfectly round potholes and wavy elongated troughs and unexpected patterns, that you could be standing at the edge of an oversize Henry Moore sculpture. The dry streambed alone would be a work of art, but at high water the beautiful shapes are still visible and become softer and even more interesting. When the water level is high, the river runs down a number of stairsteps of different widths, and near the upper part makes one free fall that could be called a true waterfall rather than a cascade, though it's very small. Once you have discovered it, it's a hard place to leave.

Height of falls: Free fall 10 feet, cascades 60 feet
Start: Dog Lake parking lot
Distance: 0.4 mile out and back
Hiking time: 20 minutes
Elevation change: Minimal
Difficulty: Easy

Seasons: Spring and summer, whenever the Tioga Road is open
Nearest facilities: Tuolumne Village
Permits: None
Maps: Vogelsang Peak and Tioga Pass, but not really needed

Finding the trailhead: From the west drive Tioga Road (CA 120) eastward past the Tuolumne Meadows Visitor Center, store, and campground, all on the right. Cross the bridge over the Tuolumne River and in a mile turn right at the entrance to the wilderness center. Follow the road as it curves around to the left for about a half mile to the Dog Lake parking lot on the left. Trailhead GPS: N37 52.39' / W119 20.20'

The Hike

From the Dog Lake parking lot, cross the road and walk a few yards downhill to meet the John Muir Trail, where you turn left (east). You will scarcely notice the Dana Fork of the Tuolumne River flowing fairly quietly alongside on your right at first. Then, after a few yards, an outcrop of granite comes between you and the river at the same time that you begin to hear the noisy splashing that indicates some boisterous water activity. Turn off the trail and make your way around or (carefully) over the rocks that hide the stream, and join the (so far) very few anglers, photographers, and sunbathers who have discovered it.

Little pools among the Dana Fork Cascades are favorites of children and anglers.

Miles and Directions

0.0 Dog Lake parking lot
0.1 John Muir Trail; turn left
0.2 View of the river is blocked by granite outcropping; scramble over this or go around
0.4 Arrive back at the trailhead

38 Young Lakes Falls

There are no gigantic waterfalls on this hike, but there are at least a dozen smaller-to-miniature cascades that fall in exquisite patterns among fabulous flower gardens. There are rugged raggedy peaks above, arising from several terraces fed by three of the bluest and most photogenic lakes anywhere. On the way are views of the whole Cathedral Range and the Sierra Crest. A perfect weekend hike. You are bound to be charmed.

Height of falls: Various
Start: Dog Lake / Lembert Dome Trailhead
Distance: 13.4 miles out and back to first lake
Hiking time: 1 day if you hurry, 2 days are better
Elevation change: 1,460 feet to the first lake
Difficulty: Strenuous as a day hike, moderate as a backpack

Seasons: All summer; whenever the Tioga Road is open
Nearest facilities: Water and supplies in Tuolumne Meadows; pit toilets at trailhead; nearest gas in Lee Vining
Permits: None for a day hike; available for overnights in advance or at the Tuolumne Meadows Wilderness Center
Maps: USGS Tioga Pass quad

Finding the trailhead: From the west drive Tioga Road (CA 120) eastward past the Tuolumne Meadows Visitor Center, store, and campground, all on the right (south). Just after crossing the bridge over the Tuolumne River, turn left into the Lembert Dome parking area. From the east (Tioga Pass) on Tioga Road, pass the turnoff to the wilderness center and Tuolumne Lodge on the left. A few hundred yards beyond, turn right into the Lembert Dome parking lot and picnic area. You can also ride the Tuolumne Meadows shuttle to Lembert Dome (stop 4). If you plan to spend the night at Young Lakes, park along the road that roughly parallels the highway. Overnight parking is prohibited in the Lembert Dome lot. Be sure to stow all food and food containers in the bear-proof boxes along the road. Trailhead GPS: N37 32.58' / W119 21.13'

The Hike

Set out northward from the "Lembert Dome / Dog Lake Trailhead" sign through lodgepole pines, crossing an open rocky slab where the route is marked by boulders. The granite has patches polished to a high sheen by glaciers. Notice the striations or scratches in the rock showing the direction in which the rivers of ice once flowed.

The trail reenters the forest, and at 0.2 mile a trail comes in from the stables to the west. A few yards beyond, a second trail from the stables joins this one. Keep straight ahead at both junctions. Climb fairly steeply alongside the sheer face of Lembert Dome, then cross a little creek as the grade becomes more gradual. At 1.0 mile keep left at a junction with the trail heading east around the back side of Lembert Dome.

The pattern of these lakes is called Paternoster since they are connected like beads on a string.

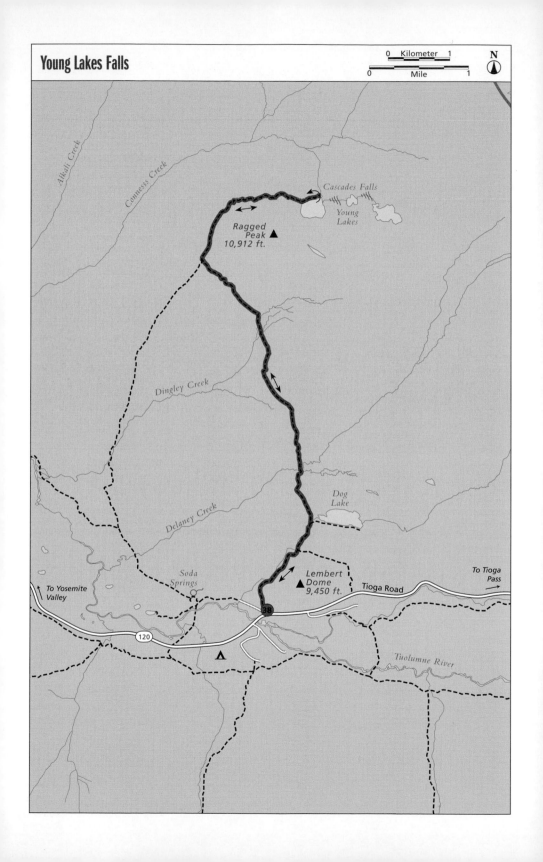

Young Lakes Falls

Alkali Creek

Conness Creek

Cascades Falls

Young Lakes

Ragged Peak
10,912 ft.

Dingley Creek

Delaney Creek

Dog Lake

Soda Springs

Lembert Dome
9,450 ft.

Tioga Road

To Tioga Pass

To Yosemite Valley

120

Tuolumne River

0 Kilometer 1

0 Mile 1

N

Ground-hugging alpine gentians prefer high-elevation meadows.

At 1.2 miles another trail cuts off to the right toward Dog Lake—it's worth a short detour especially in afternoon light. Your route continues straight ahead, crossing the outlet stream from the lake, and ascends a moderate slope for about a half mile to a pretty meadow where you hop or wade Delaney Creek. From the middle of the meadow, you can see the great red metamorphic peaks of Mount Gibbs and Mount Dana on the skyline.

Climb easily up a ridge among twisted whitebark pines for about 1.5 miles more to another meadow, where you will find one of the finest views in the entire Sierra Nevada, with the whole Cathedral Range spread out before you. There are no grand thundering cataracts nearby, but be sure to slow down to admire little Dingley Creek, sometimes trickling, sometimes rushing down among the wildflowers in a series of unnamed but exquisite miniature waterfalls. Leaving this perfect spot, the trail climbs over a sandy shoulder, the highest point on this hike, then descends to meet a junction with the Soda Springs Trail at 5.1 miles (an alternate, less scenic route back to Tuolumne Meadows). Your path turns right, continuing northward, gradually curving to the east, skirting Ragged Peak, and finally dipping into the basin containing the lowest of the three Young Lakes at 6.7 miles. You are above 9,600 feet now, so fires are prohibited. There is plenty of good camping along the western side of this first lake, but the higher lakes are equally beautiful and less crowded. Early in the

Each of the Young Lakes is connected to the others by pretty waterfalls.

season, a snowfield at the upper ends of these lakes disgorges ephemeral, but very pretty, cascades into the blue, blue water. To reach the upper lakes, follow the use trail that runs along their northern shores and scramble up alongside another set of little waterfalls that connect the lakes. These deserve every bit as much admiration as the bigger, noisier, more famous waterfalls.

From the uppermost lake you can look down upon the lower ones, with snaggle-toothed Ragged Peak jutting up behind them.

On your return to Tuolumne Meadows, you can vary your hike by keeping right (west) instead of left at the trail junction 1 mile below Young Lakes. You will end up not far from Soda Springs, where you turn left (east) to follow a dirt road back to the trailhead. This route is heavily forested all the way, so you will miss the great views of the Cathedral Range on the way down unless you return the way you came.

Miles and Directions

0.0 Dog Lake / Lembert Dome Trailhead

0.2 Trails to stables; keep right

1.0 Trail to Lembert Dome; go straight ahead

1.2 Trail to Dog Lake; keep left

5.1 Soda Springs Trail junction; turn right

6.7 First Young Lake

13.4 Arrive back at the trailhead

Hetch Hetchy
Waterfalls

Hetch Hetchy Valley occupies an out-of-the-way corner of Yosemite, but if you love waterfalls, you shouldn't miss it. The lakeside in April, May, and early June dazzles with the best display of spring wildflowers in the park, and it's a great place to hike in early season when the higher country is still under snow. It can be uncomfortably hot in midsummer. There are no commercial facilities, so it is less crowded than other parts of the park.

The Hetch Hetchy Reservoir, begun in 1919, completed in 1923, then expanded in 1938, provides water to the city of San Francisco. It has been controversial since its construction was first proposed. Yosemite is a national park, federally protected from development, and opponents insisted that other sites could have been used

Tueeulala and Wapama Falls pour into Hetch Hetchy Reservoir.

instead, but work on O'Shaughnessy Dam was begun anyway. The valley it flooded was said (and appears in old photos) to rival Yosemite itself in scenic beauty, with the Tuolumne River winding among meadows, oaks, and pines, surrounded by soaring granite cliffs and domes, and graced by several waterfalls. John Muir's famous, if fruitless, battle against the dam brought the need to preserve such wilderness treasures to the attention of the public and gave impetus to the growth of the National Park Service and to the conservation movement as a whole.

Because this reservoir provides water to a major city, it is considered vulnerable to terrorist activity. Since September 11, 2001, you must pick up a day-use permit as you pass through the entrance, display it on your car, leave the area before 9 p.m., and return the permit when you go. To protect water quality, no swimming or boating is allowed in the reservoir.

There are no public overnight accommodations at Hetch Hetchy except a walk-in campground for backpackers. You must have a wilderness permit (available at the Big Oak Flat and Hetch Hetchy entrance stations) to use it, and are limited to a one-night stay. Rangers will note your license plate number and give you a tag for your windshield marked with the date you plan to finish your backpack. The Hodgdon Meadow Campground near the Big Oak Flat entrance is the closest park campground, and reservations are recommended. There is also a concessionaire-operated Forest Service campground on Evergreen Road, and other accommodations in nearby Groveland.

To reach the Hetch Hetchy trailhead, leave CA 120 just outside the park at the Big Oak Flat Entrance Station and reenter the park at the Hetch Hetchy Entrance Station. (See individual hikes for detailed directions.)

39 Carlon Falls

This is a short but sweet and lovely hike along the South Fork of the Tuolumne River to a series of cascades and a pretty little waterfall. It's the site of a now-defunct resort known as the Carl Inn, established in 1916, destroyed by two fires, rebuilt, threatened by logging, and finally purchased by the National Park Service in the 1930s. You can still see bits of the old foundation near the beginning of the walk.

Height of falls: Indeterminate, a series of cascades; height of highest drop about 50 feet
Start: Carlon Falls Trailhead on Evergreen Road
Distance: 2.0 miles out and back
Hiking time: 1–2 hours
Elevation change: 150 feet
Difficulty: Easy with a bit of scrambling

Season: Late spring through summer
Nearest facilities: Toilets at the picnic area; water, phones, snacks at the park entrance
Permits: None
Maps: USGS Ackerson Mountain 7.5-minute quad, but the topo is out of date and useless for this hike

Finding the trailhead: Drive 1 mile west of the Big Oak Flat Entrance Station to Yosemite on CA 120. Turn right (north) on Evergreen Road and drive about a mile to a bridge over the South Fork of the Tuolumne River. There is a very small parking area at the trailhead on the right, just past the far side of the bridge. If there is no space available, there are two picnic areas with parking on either side of the river. Trailhead GPS: N37 48.52' / W119 51.42'

You can see remnants of a former resort on the path to Carlon Falls.

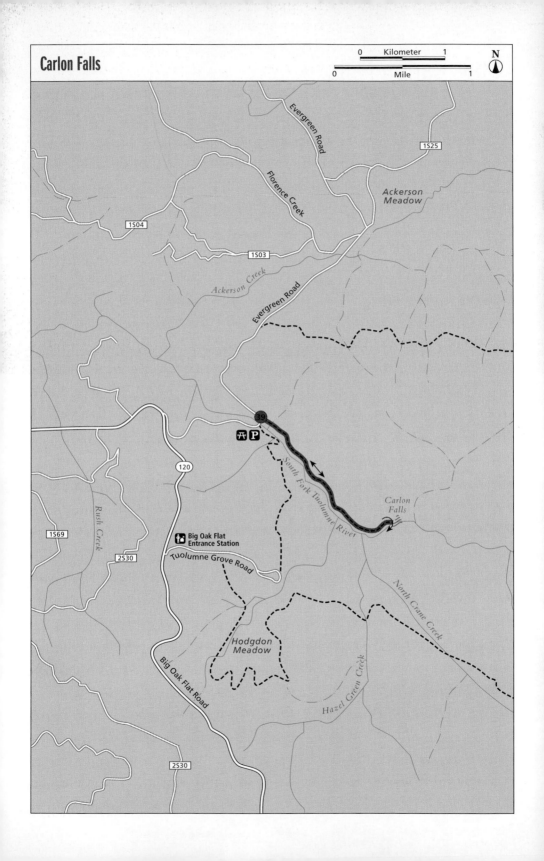

Carlon Falls

0 — Kilometer — 1

0 — Mile — 1

N

Evergreen Road

1S25

Florence Creek

Ackerson Meadow

1S04

1S03

Ackerson Creek

Evergreen Road

39

🅿 ⛲

120

South Fork Tuolumne River

Carlon Falls

Rush Creek

North Crane Creek

1S69

2S30

Big Oak Flat Entrance Station

Tuolumne Grove Road

Hodgdon Meadow

Hazel Green Creek

Big Oak Flat Road

2S30

The Carlon Falls are hidden treasures at low altitudes.

The Hike

The hike begins just outside the park border in the Stanislaus National Forest off Evergreen Road on the way to Hetch Hetchy, but you enter Yosemite after just a few steps along the trail. It is a flat, easy walk along the river most of the way, with a very short but steep section at the top. The Rim Fire of 2013 burned right up to the edge of the canyon above the upper part of the falls, and there are still quite a few downed trees across the trail, but nothing you can't duck under, step over, or go around. The scenery hasn't been spoiled in any way. Beautiful big old dogwood trees bloom in spring, and the river is home to showy patches of Indian rhubarb, also known as umbrella plant. These are tall plants with big white flowers whose big round leaves seem to be pierced through the middle by their central stalks. They grow right out of the water in showy bunches. There are pleasant pools to swim or wade in, but they can be dangerous at high water during spring snowmelt.

Miles and Directions

0.0 Carlon Falls Trailhead
0.1 Enter Yosemite
0.7 Trail starts to climb
1.0 Carlon Falls
2.0 Arrive back at the trailhead

40 Tueeulala Falls

This easy hike takes you to the first of a series of falls and cascades along the north shore of the controversial Hetch Hetchy Reservoir through what might be the finest springtime wildflower show in Yosemite. Your timing and your luck have to be good, though, since neither the falls nor the blooming period lasts very long at this 4,000-foot elevation. The winding 15-mile road through an out-of-the-way section of the park used to guarantee a bit more solitude here than elsewhere in Yosemite, but Hetch Hetchy Valley becomes busier every year. You still have a better chance of seeing a bear here, though. If you haven't had enough scenic beauty by the time you get to Tueeulala Falls, there are more falls and cascades on the trail beyond. Backpackers can continue on to meet up with more routes into the less frequently visited backcountry of the northern park from here.

Height of falls: 1,400 feet
Start: O'Shaughnessy Dam
Distance: 4.0 miles out and back
Hiking time: 2–4 hours
Elevation change: 400 feet
Difficulty: Easy
Season: Apr–June
Nearest facilities: Food and accommodations at Evergreen Lodge near Camp Mather; phones, toilets, and water near the trailhead; gas at Crane Flat
Permits: None
Maps: Lake Eleanor USGS quad

Special considerations: Make sure you know what poison oak looks like. It is easy to avoid here as long as you stay on the trail. This is also a good habitat for rattlesnakes, so watch where you put your feet. Because this reservoir provides water to a major city, it is considered vulnerable to terrorist attack. Since September 11, 2001, you must pick up a day-use permit as you enter the park, display it on your car, leave the area before 9 p.m., and return the permit when you leave. To protect water quality, no swimming or boating is allowed in the reservoir.

Finding the trailhead: Drive 1 mile west of the Big Oak Flat Entrance Station to Yosemite on CA 120. Turn right (north) on Evergreen Road and drive about 8 miles. At Camp Mather turn right (northeast) on Hetch Hetchy Road, pass through the park entrance station, then continue on for 7 miles more to where the road ends in a one-way loop. Partway around the loop is the dam and beyond is a parking area. Trailhead GPS: N37.56.48' / W119 47.14'

The Hike

Walk across the dam past some historical markers. On the far side at 0.1 mile, enjoy the troupe of acrobatic swallows swooping and diving before the entrance to a dark and dripping tunnel. Pass through the tunnel and continue along the old Lake Eleanor Road (built during construction of the dam) skirting the north shore of the

Tueeulala separates into several sections near the trail.

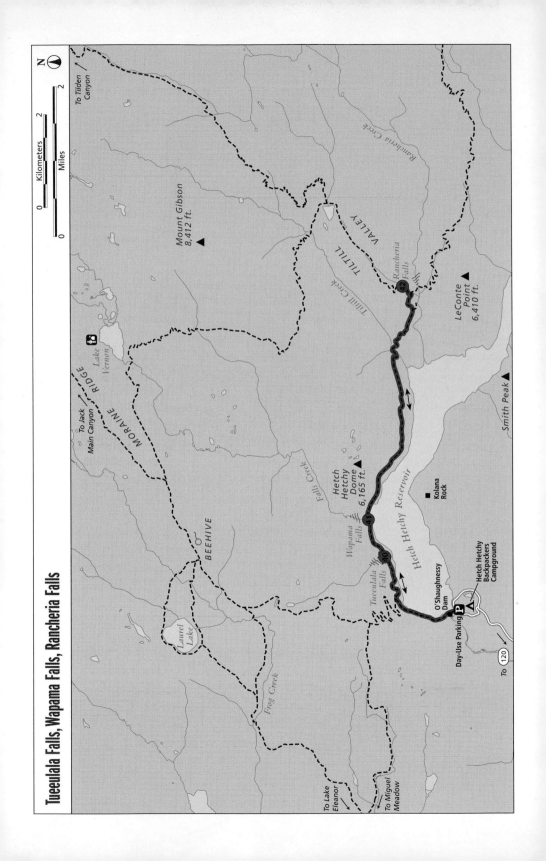

Tueeulala Falls, Wapama Falls, Rancheria Falls

N

0			2
Kilometers

0			2
Miles

To Tilden
Canyon

Rancheria Creek

Mount Gibson
8,412 ft. ▲

TILTILL VALLEY

Rancheria
Falls ②

LeConte Point
6,410 ft. ▲

Tiltill Creek

MORAINE RIDGE

To Jack
Main Canyon

Lake
Vernon

Falls Creek

Hetch
Hetchy
Dome
6,165 ft. ▲

Wapama
Falls ④

Tueeulala
Falls ⑩

Hetch Hetchy Reservoir

Kolana
Rock ■

Smith Peak ▲

BEEHIVE

Laurel
Lake

Frog Creek

To Lake
Eleanor

To Miguel
Meadow

O'Shaughnessy
Dam

Hetch Hetchy
Backpackers
Campground

Day-Use Parking P

To 120

In early spring millions of California newts rush to water to mate. MARTA KIS

lake. It is lined with live oak, bay trees, and poison oak, along with dozens of species of wildflowers, among them the unusual pink-and-yellow harlequin lupine. Little trickles of water seep from cracks in the rocks to nourish buttercups, monkey flowers, and columbines. In May, if you're lucky, you'll catch the spring migration of the little brown-and-orange California newts crossing the trail in such numbers that you must step carefully to avoid squashing them. There are other interesting reptiles along with the usual rattlesnakes, as well as gopher snakes, aquatic garter snakes, and, if you're lucky enough to see one, beautiful tricolored mountain king snakes.

The road climbs fairly gently for a while, then at 0.9 mile you reach a junction with a trail on the right where you head slightly downhill toward the lake. The road continues on upward to the left toward Lake Eleanor.

The path rises and falls and winds back and forth past more delicate little gardens, seeps, and pools on this side of the reservoir. There are lots of perfect sunny spots for lunch in the next mile overlooking the lake facing Kolana Rock brooding darkly over the opposite shore. At 2 miles Tueeulala Falls tumbles over the cliff to your left (north) and trickles down over the trail into the lake. It's not a dramatic cataract but a lovely delicate fall that separates into several sections before it crosses the trail, some with enough volume to create puddles in the trail deep enough to overtop your boots if you continue on early in the season.

Miles and Directions

0.0 O'Shaughnessy Dam
0.9 Turn right (south) onto the Wapama Falls Trail
2.0 Tueeulala Falls
4.0 Arrive back at the trailhead

41 Wapama Falls

This is a moderate springtime hike along the north shore of the controversial Hetch Hetchy Reservoir through a riotous show of springtime wildflowers The gardens are fed by several little trickles from the cliffs above, including the gentle and lovely Tueeulala Falls, worth a visit just for itself. The real excitement lies beyond amid the thunder and spray of Wapama Falls. At the height of summer snowmelt, it crashes 1,700 feet over enormous rocks, hurling itself into the lake with almost frightening and sometimes dangerous power. By midsummer the hike is hot, the falls are mostly dry, and the flowers are gone.

Height of falls: About 1,700 feet
Start: O'Shaughnessy Dam
Distance: 5.0 miles out and back
Hiking time: 3-6 hours
Elevation change: 500 feet
Difficulty: Moderate
Season: Apr-July
Nearest facilities: Food and accommodations at Evergreen Lodge; phones, toilets, and water near the trailhead; gas at Crane Flat
Permits: None
Maps: Lake Eleanor USGS quad
Special considerations: *Do not* cross the bridge over Wapama Falls if the spring runoff is at its height. The Park Service posts a sign near the trailhead at extremely high water warning that you proceed at your own risk. You can stand right beside the falls to get good photos and a thorough soaking from the spray from the west side of the bridges without crossing over. If the falls are sending water surging a foot or more deep over the top of the bridges, *stop*. There have been several fatalities here. Make sure you know what poison oak looks like. It is easy to avoid here as long as you stay on the trail. Several kinds of reptiles and amphibians including rattlesnakes live here too. Watch where you put your feet. Because this reservoir provides water to a major city, it is considered vulnerable to terrorist attack. Since September 11, 2001, you must pick up a day-use permit as you enter the park, display it on your car, leave the area before 9 p.m., and return the permit when you leave. To protect water quality, no swimming or boating is allowed in the reservoir.

Finding the trailhead: Drive 1 mile west of the Big Oak Flat Entrance Station to Yosemite on CA 120. Turn north on Evergreen Road and drive about 8 miles. At Camp Mather turn right (northeast) on Hetch Hetchy Road, pass through the park entrance station, then continue on for 7 miles more to where the road ends in a one-way loop. Partway around the loop is the dam, and just beyond is a parking area. Trailhead GPS: N37.56.48' / W119 47.14'

The Hike

Walk across the dam past some historical markers. On the far side at 0.1 mile, enjoy the troupe of acrobatic swallows swooping and diving before the entrance to a dark

It is sometimes possible to cross Wapama Falls without getting wet.

Though Wapama Falls floods its bridges, it is safe to cross at this level.

and dripping tunnel. Pass through the tunnel and continue along the old Lake Eleanor Road, built during construction of the dam, skirting the north shore of the lake. It's lined with live oak, bay trees, and poison oak, along with dozens of species of wildflowers, among them the seldom seen pink-and-yellow harlequin lupine. Little trickles of water seep from cracks in the rocks to nourish buttercups, monkey flowers, and columbines. In May, if you're lucky, you'll catch the spring migration of the little brown-and-orange California newts crossing the trail in such numbers that you must step carefully to avoid squashing them.

The road climbs fairly gently for a while, then at 0.9 mile you reach a junction with a trail on the right where you head slightly downhill toward the lake. The

Flying spray makes Wapama Falls look even bigger than it is.

road continues on upward to the left toward Lake Eleanor. The path rises and falls and curves back and forth past delicate little gardens, seeps, and pools, while on the opposite side of the reservoir, Kolana Rock broods darkly over the south shore. At 2 miles Tueeulala Falls tumbles over the cliff to your left and trickles down over the trail into the lake. It's not a massive, forceful fall but a delicate flow that separates into several strands before it crosses the trail, some of them deep enough to get your feet wet until mid-June. The trail continues along the cliff above the lake, climbing and descending now and then until, at 2.5 miles, you'll feel the spray and hear the thunder of the waters of Wapama Falls. Toward the bottom (though still far above the level of the lake), the falls split into several sections, each of which is crossed on a separate footbridge. If water is flowing over the tops of the bridges, test its depth and the strength of the current with your first step onto each one before striding across. You can expect a refreshing shower in the middle. The density of the spray can make photography an interesting challenge here. Return to the trailhead.

Miles and Directions

- **0.0** O'Shaughnessy Dam
- **0.1** Tunnel
- **0.9** Trail/road junction; turn right onto the trail
- **2.0** Tueeulala Falls
- **2.5** Wapama Falls
- **5.0** Arrive back at the trailhead

42 Rancheria Falls

Rancheria Fall itself is a small but dramatic waterfall at the head of a series of exuberant cascades alternating with perfect swimming holes. The Rancheria Campground is the first place you can camp along the reservoir, and it is a popular and beautiful spot. The hike there can be hot and tiring, but there are two other stunning falls for you to pause, rest, and admire along the way, at least one of which is guaranteed to provide a refreshing shower. It's a great place for wildlife too. Don't forget your bear canister.

Height of falls: 25 feet, ending in a series of cascades
Start: O'Shaughnessy Dam
Distance: 14.4 miles out and back
Hiking time: 6 hours to 2 days
Elevation change: 1,400 feet
Difficulty: Moderate as a backpack, strenuous as a day hike
Season: Apr–June
Nearest facilities: Food and accommodations at Evergreen Lodge near Camp Mather; phones, toilets, and water near the trailhead; gas at Crane Flat
Permits: None for a day hike. Available for overnights in advance or at the Hetch Hetchy Entrance Station.

Maps: USGS Hetch Hetchy Reservoir and Lake Eleanor quads
Special considerations: Make sure you know what poison oak looks like. It is very easy to avoid here as long as you stay on the trail. It is also at a low enough and warm enough elevation for rattlesnakes, so watch where you put your feet. Because this reservoir provides water to a major city, it is considered vulnerable to terrorist attack. Since September 11, 2001, if you will be backpacking, rangers will note your car license number and give you a hangtag for your rearview mirror or dashboard with your expected date of return. To protect water quality, no swimming or boating is allowed in the reservoir.

Finding the trailhead: Drive 1 mile west of the Big Oak Flat Entrance Station to Yosemite on CA 120. Turn right (north) on Evergreen Road and drive about 8 miles. At Camp Mather turn right (northeast) on Hetch Hetchy Road, pass through the park entrance station, then continue on for 7 miles more to where the road ends in a one-way loop. At the beginning of the loop, turn left on a spur road for backpackers parking, with a big collection of bear boxes where you can store food you won't be carrying with you. Just beyond this is the backpackers camp. If you are in very good condition and plan to hike to Rancheria Fall and back on the same day, continue to drive around the loop to the dam, just beyond which you'll find day-use parking. Trailhead GPS: N37.56.48' / W119 47.14'

The Hike

Walk across the dam past some historical markers. On the far side at 0.1 mile, enjoy the troupe of acrobatic swallows swooping and diving before the entrance to a dark and dripping tunnel. Pass through the tunnel and continue along the level road

The campground is just alongside the cascades and handy pools.

skirting the north shore of the lake; it's lined with live oak, bay trees, and poison oak, along with dozens of species of wildflowers, among them the unusual pink-and-yellow harlequin lupine. Little trickles of water seep from cracks in the rocks to nourish buttercups, monkey flowers, and columbines. In May, if you're lucky, you'll catch the spring migration of the little brown-and-orange California newts crossing the trail in such numbers that you must step carefully to avoid squashing them.

There are other interesting reptiles along with the rattlesnakes, among them the nonpoisonous aquatic garter snake, and, if you are lucky, the beautiful mountain king snake.

The road climbs fairly gently for a while, then at 0.9 mile you reach a junction with a trail on the right where you head slightly downhill toward the lake. The path rises and falls and curves back and forth past delicate little gardens, seeps, and pools here while on the opposite side Kolana Rock broods darkly over the south shore. At 2 miles Tueeualala Falls tumbles down over the cliff to the left and trickles over the trail into the lake. Early in the season you'll probably get your feet wet, though it's usually dry by mid-June. Continue along the cliff above the lake, climbing and

▶ A *rancheria* is a (sometimes seasonal) settlement where native people gathered to collect and prepare acorns, a staple food along with seeds of grasses, one of which was called hetch hetchy. Stay on the lookout for scattered bedrock mortars, granite rocks where Miwok women pounded acorns in shallow cuplike holes in the rocks. They are most often found beside streams where the tannin could be leached from the acorn meal.

Tiny butterflies gather in shallow ponds to consume important minerals.

descending, until at 2.5 miles you will hear the thunder and feel the spray of Wapama Falls. Pick your way across the several bridges that span the multiple strands of the falls, sometimes sloshing through deep water, sometimes bracing yourself against potentially dangerous torrents, sometime strolling by with perfectly dry feet. *Turn back if the water flowing over the bridge is more than upper-shin deep.* The trail gains some elevation above the lake and makes its way around Hetch Hetchy Dome. Occasional patches of shady oak forest alternate with stretches of sunny, sweaty trudging until the trail crosses an unnamed creek on a little bridge, rounds a corner, and crosses more substantial Tiltill Creek on a bigger one. Finally, after one last hot, shadeless climb, you top out on a shoulder from which there is a good view of Rancheria Creek roaring down a series of waterslides to the reservoir. About a quarter mile beyond, at 6.9 miles, a sign marks the turnoff to the camping area near the river on your right.

If you are spending the night, find a campsite first. This is a popular spot. Now continue on the trail past the campground, keeping to the right at a junction with the trail to Tiltill Valley about a quarter mile up. Just around the corner, at mile 7.3, a bridge over Rancheria Creek spans a rocky gorge where the stream is squeezed into the neck of a narrow funnel and drops in a 25-foot fall, sending the creek water in a boiling, foaming rush down into the lake.

Miles and Directions

0.0 O'Shaughnessy Dam

0.9 Trail/road junction; turn right onto the trail

2.5 Wapama Falls

6.9 Rancheria Falls Campground

7.1 Junction with Tiltill Valley Trail; keep right

7.3 Top of Rancheria Falls

14.6 Arrive back at the trailhead

43 Lake Vernon Cascade

Lake Vernon is the source of Falls Creek, which in early season feeds Hetch Hetchy's spectacular Tueeulala and Wapama Falls. The outlet to the lake roars down in cascades and little waterwheels at first, then slides out of sight. It is definitely a seasonal fall. Lake Vernon is lovely anytime, but the fall is only a dribble after mid-June. Only a few of the little trickles you pass on your way up might have water, but the first reliable source is the spring at Beehive.

Height of fall: Indeterminate
Start: O'Shaughnessy Dam
Distance: 20.6 miles out and back
Hiking time: 2–3 days
Elevation change: 3,600 feet
Difficulty: Moderate
Season: Apr to mid-June
Nearest facilities: Food and accommodations at Evergreen Lodge; toilets, phones, water near the trailhead; gas at Crane Flat
Permits: Required. Available in advance or from the Hetch Hetchy or Big Oak Flat entrance stations.

Maps: USGS Lake Eleanor, Kibbie Lake, Tiltill Mountain quads
Special considerations: Carry plenty of water if you begin this hike after early June. The only truly reliable sources in a dry year are Beehive and Lake Vernon. Because this reservoir provides water to a major city, it is considered vulnerable to terrorist attack. Since September 11, 2001, if you will be backpacking, rangers will note your car license number and give you a hangtag for your rearview mirror or dashboard with your expected date of return. To protect water quality, no swimming or boating is allowed in the reservoir.

Finding the trailhead: Drive 1 mile west of the Big Oak Flat Entrance Station to Yosemite on CA 120. Turn right (north) on Evergreen Road and drive about 8 miles. At Camp Mather turn right (northeast) on Hetch Hetchy Road, pass through the park entrance station, then continue on for 7 miles more to where the road ends in a one-way loop. At the beginning of the loop, turn left on a spur road for backpackers parking, with a big collection of bear boxes where you can store food you won't be carrying with you. Just beyond this is the backpackers camp. Walk either direction along the loop road to the dam. Trailhead GPS: N37 56.48' / W119 47.14'

The Hike

Walk across the dam past some historical markers and on through a dark and dripping tunnel to emerge into sunlight on the old Lake Eleanor Road, lined with live oak, bay trees, and poison oak, along with dozens of species of wildflowers. At 0.9 mile a trail cuts away from the road, heading to the right toward the reservoir. Stay on the road and climb the long, partly shaded switchbacks to a junction with a trail to Miguel Meadow at 3.6 miles. Keep right (north) and ascend beneath pines and incense cedars to a more level stretch that winds through an open rocky area lined with manzanita.

Sometimes in early season the path to the bridge is underwater.

Reenter partly burned forest and climb past a couple of tiny emerald-green meadows carpeted with white meadow foam and yellow monkey flowers.

Now, labor up a steep forested slope to what seems to be an oddly placed oblong unnamed lake (on top of a ridge). Pass through an open section with a pure stand of prickly ceanothus, then turn a corner and reenter forest lined with dense bracken fern. Pass a junction to Lake Eleanor at 6.0 miles and keep right (north) again. At 6.8 miles you reach Beehive, a soggy, mosquito-ridden but flower-filled meadow where there is a piped spring protected by wood planks. (The water should be purified before drinking.) Another path goes west to Laurel Lake from here. Keep right, climbing steeply at one point to reach yet another junction at 8.1 miles with the Wilma Lake Trail toward Jack Main Canyon, heading northeast to the top of Moraine Ridge.

Follow the right fork for a time, then drop down an open rocky slope and cross over a low hump to enter the Lake Vernon basin. Before you start the downward drop, if you are early enough, you cross some little trickles surrounding miniature islands of soil blooming with solid carpets of yellow monkey flowers. To your right the larger of these trickles takes a long beautiful slide down and out of sight. It's a lovely landscape, dotted with artistically placed pines and junipers. Climb a little more, then drop down into the Lake Vernon basin. Just before you reach the lake, there is a sign that says "0.1 mile to Lake Vernon," pointing to the left. Go right 0.1 to 0.2 mile toward Tiltill Valley to the bridge that crosses Falls Creek. The stream begins

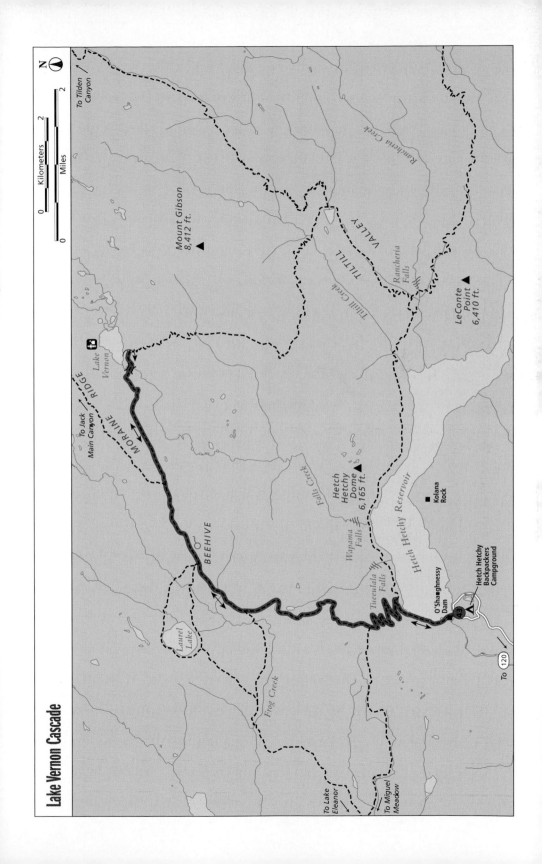

Lake Vernon Cascade

N

Kilometers
0   2

Miles
0   2

To Tilden Canyon

Rancheria Creek

Mount Gibson
8,412 ft.

TILTIL VALLEY

Tiltil Creek

Rancheria Falls

LeConte Point
6,410 ft.

Falls Creek

MORAINE RIDGE

To Jack Main Canyon

Lake Vernon

Hetch Hetchy Dome
6,165 ft.

BEEHIVE

Wapama Falls

Hetch Hetchy Reservoir

Kolana Rock

Laurel Lake

Tueeulala Falls

O'Shaughnessy Dam

Hetch Hetchy Backpackers Campground

Frog Creek

To Lake Eleanor

To Miguel Meadow

To 120

Lake Vernon, the source of Falls Creek, feeds Wapama Falls.

its descent right under your feet on the bridge that crosses it. It's not a precipitous fall but mostly a cascade, followed by a slide, but the best part is right under the bridge you're standing on, where Falls Creek begins its descent down to Wapama Falls, and ultimately Hetch Hetchy Reservoir. At high water there are a couple of little waterwheels almost right under the bridge.

If you decide to stay at the lake, the best camping is on the rock slabs on the southwest side. Return the way you came, or you can continue along the traditional "loop" that takes you south to Tiltill Valley, over Tiltill Creek, on down to Rancheria Falls, then back along Hetch Hetchy Reservoir past Wapama and Tueeulala Falls back to the dam, a 26.7-mile popular loop. You can do it in either direction.

Miles and Directions

0.0 O'Shaughnessy Dam

0.9 Keep left, climbing old Lake Eleanor Road

3.6 Junction with the trail to Miguel Meadow; keep right

6.0 Continue straight ahead at a junction with the trail to Lake Eleanor

6.8 Beehive Meadow

8.1 Junction with Wilma Lake Trail; keep right toward Lake Vernon

10.1 Junction at the outlet stream from Lake Vernon; turn right

10.2 Bridge over the Lake Vernon Cascade

20.6 Arrive back at the trailhead

Grand Canyon of the Tuolumne River Waterfalls

The Tuolumne is one of Yosemite's two major rivers. (The other is the Merced.) The Lyell Fork of the Tuolumne originates at the glacier on Mount Lyell; the Dana Fork flows from the snowfields of Mount Dana. The two forks meet in Tuolumne Meadows where the now-swollen river wanders languorously northwest for a few miles, then begins its headlong rush toward the Pacific in an almost continuous series of cascades and waterfalls until it is interrupted by O'Shaughnessy Dam, the source of San Francisco's drinking water.

Hiking all or part of this canyon is the well-conditioned waterfall lovers' ultimate adventure. Once you enter the gorge, the world outside becomes remote and inconsequential. The Tuolumne River (and the trail) drop nearly 5,000 feet in about

The Lyell Glacier is the source of the water that deepens the canyon.

177

30 miles, descending alongside cascade after cascade, waterfall after waterfall, sliding into sometimes roiling, sometimes swimmable pools, depending on the time of year. The walls of the canyon are almost vertical and rise many hundreds of feet above the valley floor, and countless unnamed tributary streams pour over the rim to bring even more waterfalls down to meet the river.

You don't have to commit to hiking the gorge end to end. There are a number of easy-to-strenuous day hikes to one or more of the waterfalls created by the Tuolumne, or you can tackle a multiday backpack from one end to the other. If you're lucky enough to score a reservation, you can spend a night at Glen Aulin High Sierra Camp right beside the White Cascade, or in the backpackers campground just beyond. There are good campsites beyond these as well. You can enter the canyon at either end, from Tuolumne Meadows at 8,600 feet, or from White Wolf at 7,900 feet, but either way you can expect lots of elevation change. The trail reaches its lowest point in the gorge at Pate Valley, a little above 4,000 feet.

Applying for a wilderness backpacking permit can be tricky since it's impossible to know in advance when the Tioga Road will be open and whether early-season stream crossings will be safe or even possible. On the other hand, if you start too late, some of the big falls will have lost much of their pizzazz, some of the smaller ones will be dry, and temperatures at the lower elevations may be uncomfortably hot. Still, any veteran of this canyon will tell you it's worth the gamble whenever you go.

Finally, all the hikes here will either be out-and-back or will require a significant car shuttle. There really aren't any convenient loops.

44 Tuolumne Falls and the White Cascade

There are more scenic wonders along the trail to Glen Aulin than on any other route below the high alpine zone anywhere in Yosemite. For most of its length, it follows the course of the Tuolumne River as it wanders through meadows beneath the domes and spires of the Cathedral Range, then rushes and tumbles down in cascade after cascade as the canyon steepens and narrows to form Tuolumne Falls, a perfect place for a lunch stop. If you have the desire and the energy for more, you can continue fairly steeply down less than a mile to Glen Aulin and the White Cascade. The hike ends at the most idyllic setting imaginable, where the glorious White Cascade feeds a beautifully proportioned pool in front of the Glen Aulin High Sierra Camp. You're not likely to find solitude here since this is part of the High Sierra loop as well as the Pacific Crest Trail, with a High Sierra Camp and a backpackers campground.

Height of falls: Tuolumne Fall, 100 feet; White Cascade, 75 feet
Start: Tuolumne Meadows
Distance: 11.2 miles out and back
Hiking time: 6–7 hours or overnight
Elevation change: 800 feet
Difficulty: Easy as a backpack, moderate as a day hike
Seasons: All summer, whenever the Tioga Road is open

Nearest facilities: Tuolumne Meadows Store, Grill, just west of the Tuolumne Meadows Campground. Gas at Crane Flat and Lee Vining. Toilets but no water at trailhead.
Permits: None for a day hike, available for overnights in advance or at the Tuolumne Meadows Wilderness Center. None if you have scored a reservation at the High Sierra Camp.
Maps: USGS Falls Ridge and Tioga Pass quads

Finding the trailhead: From the west follow the Tioga Road (CA 120) past the Tuolumne Meadows Visitor Center, store, cafe, and campground, all on your right. Just after crossing the bridge over the Tuolumne River, turn left (north) into the Lembert Dome parking lot. From the east (Tioga Pass), follow the Tioga Pass Road past the turnoff to the wilderness center on your left and continue about 0.2 mile to the Lembert Dome parking area on your right. Overnight parking is prohibited in the parking lot, so if you are planning to backpack, park along the paved road parallel to Tioga Road. It turns right at a closed gate, where your hike begins. Trailhead GPS: N37 52.44' / W119 21.30'

The Hike

Go through the gate and follow the road (closed to vehicles) westward through the meadow, keeping right and climbing a small rise where the road splits. From the top of the rise, head toward the ramshackle log structure partially containing Soda Springs at mile 0.5, a naturally carbonated spring bubbling up rusty water. Just beyond that is Parsons Lodge, a stone building with historical exhibits. The path splits in front of the building at mile 0.6. Turn right. In just a few paces is a big sign

Tuolumne Falls and the White Cascade

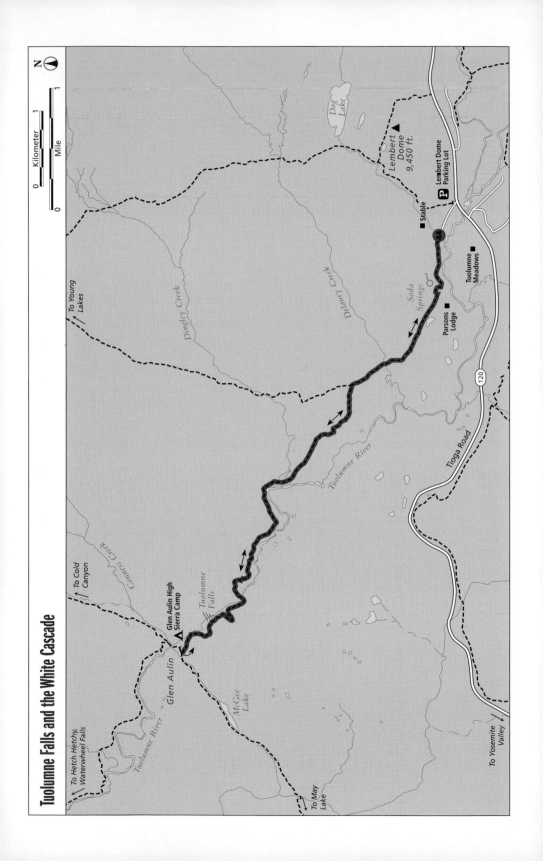

Tuolumne Falls is the first significant drop in the Grand Canyon of the Tuolumne.

The Little Devil's Postpile is an unusual volcanic formation that's younger than the surrounding rock.

marking the trail to Glen Aulin. Walk through flowery meadows and lodgepole pine forest to ford Delaney Creek at 1.2 miles.

At 1.6 miles meet a junction with a trail that heads north to Young Lakes. Continue northwest, descending very gradually. You emerge from behind a low ridge to behold the spectacular Cathedral Range with the Tuolumne River in the foreground. The next couple of miles offer one irresistible photo op after another. Sometimes the trail passes over highly polished granite, buffed to a blinding sheen by rivers of ice. Follow the ducks across these open spaces to stay on the trail. When the path climbs above the river around a shoulder of rock, keep a lookout downhill to your left to see the Little Devil's Postpile, an unusual volcanic formation that is much younger than the surrounding rock. From here you turn sharply right and drop down a short, steep notch where you very soon reach a pair of footbridges across the Tuolumne River at 4 miles.

From this point on, the river picks up speed and cascades over a series of rocky ledges, one after another, all the way to Tuolumne Falls, where the cliffs squeeze together to force the river into a perfectly formed double-decker cataract, conveniently close to the trail for great photos any time of day. The trail alternately dives into and out of deep forest lined with Labrador tea and corn lily, then emerges again into sunlight on cobblestones or smooth granite marked with ducks. As you continue to descend, watch for a grand view up Cold Canyon to Matterhorn Peak and Mount Conness at the northern boundary of Yosemite. At a junction with the May Lake Trail at 5.3 miles, turn sharply right and descend a few more steep, slippery switchbacks to the bridge back over the Tuolumne. You will surely want to pause for pictures of the frothy White Cascade, which splashes into a perfect pool in front of Glen Aulin High Sierra Camp. To reach

The White Cascade feeds the pool in front of Glen Aulin High Sierra Camp.

the camp and the backpackers campground behind it, cross a second bridge over Cold Creek to your right.

Miles and Directions

- **0.0** Glen Aulin Trailhead
- **0.5** Soda Springs
- **0.6** Parsons Lodge and trail sign; turn right, then left
- **1.2** Ford Delaney Creek
- **1.6** Young Lakes Trail junction; keep left
- **4.0** Cross the twin bridges over the Tuolumne; turn right (downstream)
- **4.5** Tuolumne Falls
- **5.3** May Lake Trail junction; turn sharp right
- **5.6** Glen Aulin High Sierra Camp
- **11.2** Arrive back at the trailhead

45 Waterwheel Falls via LeConte and California Falls

A Tuolumne River extravaganza, a moderate backpack to the White Cascade at Glen Aulin for a two-night stay at the Glen Aulin backpackers camp. If you're lucky enough, you might score a reservation for a tent cabin and meals at the Glen Aulin High Sierra Camp (available by lottery). On your layover day from either place, descend a fairly steep trail 3.3 miles each way to three more of Yosemite's most famous and dramatic waterfalls: California Falls, LeConte Falls, and the Waterwheels.

Heights of falls: California Falls 120 feet, LeConte 250 feet, Waterwheels 700 feet
Start: Tuolumne Meadows
Distance: 17.8 miles out and back
Hiking time: 6-9 hours or overnight
Elevation change: 4,000 feet
Difficulty: Moderate as a backpack, strenuous as a day hike
Seasons: All summer, whenever the Tioga Road is open, but all the falls are best as early in the season as possible
Nearest facilities: Food, water, phones, toilets at Tuolumne Meadows. Water, toilet, and a few emergency supplies at Glen Aulin. Gas at Lee Vining and Crane Flat.

Permits: None for a day hike. Available in advance or from the Tuolumne Meadows Wilderness Center for overnights.
Maps: Falls Ridge, Tioga Pass
Special considerations: The waterfalls are at their finest in July, but if there has been a late snowfall, the Tioga Road to Tuolumne Meadows might not be open and stream crossings may be difficult. In record years of high snowfall, the Tioga Road has not opened until August and the High Sierra Camp did not open at all. If you wait until August or later, the Tuolumne River will still be flowing and the falls still falling, but neither LeConte nor the Waterwheels will be at their best.

Finding the trailhead: From the west follow the Tioga Road (CA 120) past the Tuolumne Meadows Visitor Center, store, cafe, and campground, all on your right. Just after crossing the bridge over the Tuolumne River, turn left (north) into the Lembert Dome parking lot. From the east (Tioga Pass), follow the Tioga Pass Road past the turnoff to the wilderness center on your left and continue about 0.2 mile to the Lembert Dome parking lot on your right. Overnight parking is prohibited in the parking lot, so if you are planning to backpack, park along the paved road parallel to Tioga Road. It turns right at a closed gate, where your hike begins. Trailhead GPS: N37 52.44' / W119 21.30'

The Hike

The first part of this hike follows the Pacific Crest Trail. Go through the gate and follow the road (closed to vehicles) westward through the meadow, keeping right and climbing a small rise, and head toward the ramshackle log structure partially containing Soda Springs at mile 0.5. Soda Springs is a naturally carbonated spring that

California Falls is the first big cascade in the Grand Canyon of the Tuolumne.

bubbles up rusty water. Just beyond is Parsons Lodge, a stone building with historical exhibits. The path splits in front of the cabin at mile 0.6. Turn right.

The trail to Glen Aulin, marked by a big sign, meets the road a few yards beyond. Turn left this time. Walk through flowery meadows and lodgepole pine forest on footing that is heavy and dusty since pack trains going to and from the High Sierra Camp use the path too. Ford Delaney Creek at mile 1.2—it's usually shallow enough to wade. At 1.6 miles meet a junction with one of the trails that heads north to Young Lakes. Continue northwest, descending very gradually. In less than a mile, you emerge from behind a low ridge to behold the spectacular Cathedral Range with the Tuolumne River in the foreground. The next couple of miles offer one photo op after another. Sometimes the trail passes over highly polished granite buffed by glacial ice to a blinding sheen. Follow the ducks across these open spaces to stay on the trail. Climb around a low shoulder of rock and keep watch on your left for the Little Devil's Postpile, an unusual volcanic feature that's much younger than the surrounding rock.

The trail turns sharply right and drops down a short, steep notch and very soon reaches a pair of footbridges across the Tuolumne River at 4 miles. From this point on, the river picks up speed and cascades over a series of falls, one after another, all the way to Glen Aulin. One of these, Tuolumne Falls, is close enough to the trail for hikers to feel the spray. Continue descending, enjoying views up Cold Canyon to Matterhorn Peak and Mount Conness on the northern boundary of the park. The

Waterwheel Falls via LeConte and California Falls

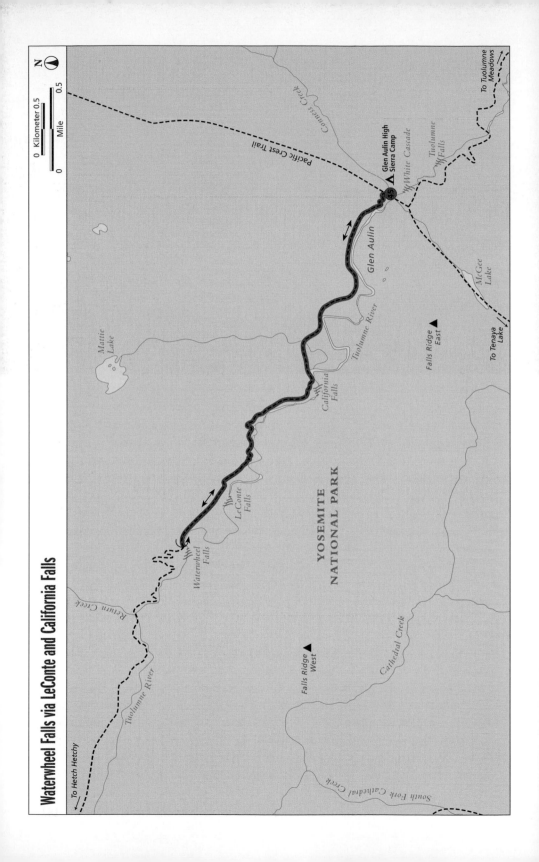

LeConte is often confused with Waterwheels, since both have waterwheels.

trail dives into and out of deep forest lined with Labrador tea and corn lily, then emerges again into sunlight on cobblestones or smooth granite marked with ducks. Finally it meets a junction with the May Lake Trail at 5 miles. A few more steep, slippery switchbacks lead down to a bridge and back to the other side of the river. Few hikers can resist the urge to stop on the bridge and snap a photo or simply gape at the frothy White Cascade splashing into a pool in front of Glen Aulin High Sierra Camp. You have come 5.2 miles, and this is where you part company with the Pacific Crest Trail.

To reach the camp, cross a second bridge to the right over Cold Creek. North-ward, behind the camp, is a backpackers campground with bear boxes and a solar composting toilet. The campground is much bigger than it looks as it is divided into three separate sections on terraces one above the other. Each section has a group fire ring to be shared with other campers. Do not build a new one.

To continue on to more waterfalls, cross the bridge back over Cold Creek to the west side, climb over a ridge, and wander through a waist-high field of lupines that have flourished since Glen Aulin was burned years ago. Some people still do camp in Glen Aulin to avoid the crowds at the High Sierra Camp, but they must camp more than 100 feet from the river. In another mile both trail and river drop over a long series of stairsteps down past California Falls, a beautiful series of cascades, then past LeConte Falls, which does form its own set of waterwheels, then on to the official Waterwheels themselves. Here the river rushes down a smooth slope until it hits a

The Tuolumne flows more quietly for a time below the Waterwheels.

series of grooves in the rocks that sometimes fling the water more than 20 feet into the air in a series of huge arcs. Watch for a little unmarked spur trail leading toward the bottom of the falls for a better view, but do not walk out onto the slippery rock beside the water, especially if it is wet. Slimy algae on polished rock is slick as glass, and a slip could be fatal.

There are more long, scenic cascades farther down the river, but none as exciting as these, and the trail gets hotter, steeper, and rockier beyond. Make sure you leave time to return to the camp or the trailhead.

Miles and Directions

0.0   Glen Aulin Trailhead
0.5   Soda Springs
0.6   Parsons Lodge and trail sign; turn right, then left
1.2   Ford Delaney Creek
1.6   Young Lakes Trail junction; keep left
4.0   Cross the twin bridges over the Tuolumne; turn right (downstream)
5.3   May Lake Trail junction; turn sharp right
5.6   Glen Aulin High Sierra Camp
7.6   California Falls
8.3   Le Conte Falls
8.9   Waterwheel Falls
17.8   Arrive back at the trailhead

46 The Grand Canyon of the Tuolumne

This is a multiday shuttle hike following the course of the Tuolumne River downstream as it tumbles over more cascades and waterfalls than you can count, including the famous Waterwheels. It travels through the Grand Canyon of the Tuolumne almost as far as Hetch Hetchy Reservoir. The route drops from 8,600 feet down to 4,200 feet before laboring back up to White Wolf at 7,900 feet. It's a wild, exhilarating hike for waterfall lovers in good condition. It does require a significant car shuttle or a ride on the Tuolumne Meadows bus. You can do this hike in the opposite direction, starting at White Wolf and climbing to Tuolumne, but most hikers prefer downhill.

Height of falls: Various
Start: Tuolumne Meadows
Distance: 29.1 miles one way/shuttle
Hiking time: 3–5 days
Elevation change: 7,000 feet
Difficulty: Strenuous
Season: Early July is best for full-flowing falls

Nearest facilities: Tuolumne Meadows; snacks and phones at White Wolf
Permits: Required; available in advance or from the Tuolumne Meadows Wilderness Center
Maps: USGS Falls Ridge, Hetch Hetchy Reservoir, Tamarack Flat, Ten Lakes, and Tioga Pass quads

Finding the trailhead: From the west follow Tioga Road (CA 120) past the Tuolumne Meadows Visitor Center, store, cafe, and campground, all on the right. Just after crossing the bridge over the Tuolumne River, turn left (north) into the Lembert Dome parking lot. From the east (Tioga Pass), follow Tioga Road past the turnoff to the wilderness center on the left and continue a mile to the Lembert Dome parking lot on the right. You can also ride the Tuolumne Meadows Shuttle to Lembert Dome (stop 4).

Overnight parking is prohibited in the parking lot, so park along the paved road parallel to Tioga Road. At a closed gate this road turns sharply right and heads toward the stables. The trail begins at the gate. Trailhead GPS: N37 52.44' / W119 21.30'

The Hike

Go through the gate and follow the road (closed to vehicles) westward through the meadow, keeping right and climbing a small rise where the road splits, then head toward the ramshackle log structure partially containing Soda Springs at mile 0.5. Soda Springs is a naturally carbonated spring that bubbles up rusty water. Just beyond is Parsons Lodge, a stone building with historical exhibits. There the path splits at mile 0.6, where you turn right to a big Glen Aulin Trail sign where the trail meets the road a few yards beyond. Turn left and walk through meadow and lodgepole pine forest on footing that is heavy and dusty from lots of horse and foot traffic. Ford Delaney Creek at mile 1.2. A trail heading north to Young Lakes cuts off to the right at mile 1.6, but your route stays left (northwest). In less than a mile of gradual

The Tuolumne River falls in continuous cascades, many of them unnamed.

descent, you emerge from behind a low ridge to behold the spectacular Cathedral Range with the Tuolumne River in the foreground. Sometimes the trail passes over polished granite, buffed by glacial ice to a blinding sheen, and you will need to watch for ducks across the open spaces to stay on track. After passing through another short stretch of forest, climb around a low shoulder of rock and keep watch on your left for the Little Devil's Postpile, an unusual volcanic feature that's much younger than the surrounding rock.

The trail turns sharply right and drops down a short, steep notch and very soon reaches a pair of footbridges across the Tuolumne River at 4.0 miles. From this point on, the river picks up speed and cascades over a series of falls, one after another. As you descend, you can enjoy views up Cold Canyon to Matterhorn Peak and Mount Conness on the northern boundary of the park. The trail twice dives into and out of deep forest lined with Labrador tea and corn lily, then emerges again into sunlight on cobblestones or smooth granite marked with ducks. Finally, it meets the May Lake / McGee Lake Trail at 5.3 miles. A few more steep, slippery switchbacks lead down to a bridge and back to the other side of the river. Few hikers can resist the urge to stop and snap a photo or simply gape at the frothy White Cascade splashing into a pool in front of the Glen Aulin High Sierra Camp at 5.6 miles. If you plan to camp here, cross a second bridge over Cold Creek to the right and walk behind the High Sierra Camp to find the backpackers campground. This is where your route leaves the Pacific Crest Trail, which continues northward along Cold Creek.

The Grand Canyon of the Tuolumne

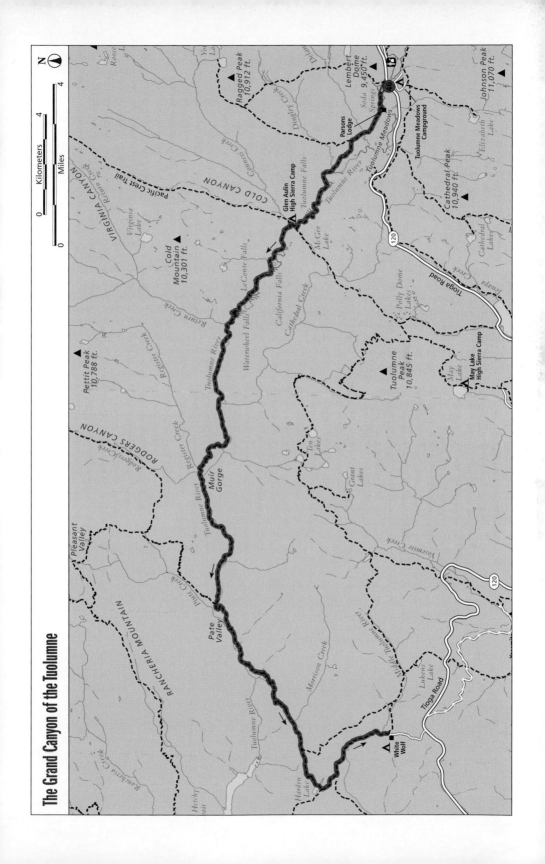

Hikers are grateful for this bridge over boisterous Return Creek.

From the camp cross back over to the west side of Cold Creek, climb over a ridge, and descend into the burned-over glen, where you wander for a mile through a waist-high sea of lupine. The river flows quiet and deep beside you for a while, then both trail and river drop over the first of a long series of stairsteps, down past California Falls, LeConte Falls, and finally the famous Waterwheels, at 8.9 miles. Here in early season the roaring Tuolumne rushes down a smooth slope until it hits a series of grooves in the rocks that sometimes fling the water more than 20 feet into the air. Watch for a little spur trail leading toward the riverside for a better view, but do not walk out onto the slippery rock beside the water, especially if the rock is wet. The combination of slimy algae on polished rock creates a surface as slick as glass, and a slip could be fatal.

Return to the main trail and continue to switchback down (and occasionally up) a brutal section of trail with no shade and no access to water until you reach Return Creek at mile 10.2. Cross the bridge and pass through dense forest where the canyon walls narrow. The slope becomes so precipitous at Muir Gorge that the trail must make a detour over the top of a smooth shoulder. It then drops steeply into the drainage of Register Creek, which you cross on rocks below a pretty cascade at mile 14.7. A little farther on, cross Rodgers Creek on a bridge. Now that you are well into the zone of black oak and chaparral, the canyon can be hot and the flies voracious. Stay alert for rattlesnakes as well. Fortunately, there are lots of inviting little

◄ *Return Creek would be a difficult crossing without the bridge.*

pools alternating with lovely cascades for cooling off. As you approach Pate Valley, the ground becomes soggier and you wade through dense bracken fern and leopard lilies until at mile 20.5 you meet a junction with a trail that heads up Piute Creek to Pleasant Valley. Cross bridges over two branches of the river to its south side and enter Pate Valley proper. There are good campsites here along the river beneath shady oaks and ponderosa pines, where masses of white azaleas scent the air in June. This is a good place to spend the night no matter what time you arrive, because the climb up out of the canyon can be very hot and should be tackled early in the morning. Make sure you have plenty of water if it is past mid-July since Morrison Creek, the only stream you will meet on your way up, is sometimes dry by then.

Leave the river and begin the trudge up the switchbacks, eventually getting high enough to look back upon Hetch Hetchy Reservoir down the canyon. After the first set of switchbacks, cross Morrison Creek in a cool aspen grove. (You might have to wade in early season, though later the creek can be completely dry.) Climb another set of switchbacks alongside the creek. At 26.7 miles pass the first junction with a shortcut trail to Harden Lake and continue straight ahead (west), climbing less steeply at first, then mounting a last set of switchbacks to Harden Lake (no camping allowed) at 28.2 miles. From the lake follow the fire road back up to White Wolf at 29.1 miles.

Miles and Directions

0.0 Glen Aulin Trailhead

0.5 Soda Springs

0.6 Parsons Lodge; turn right, then left at the sign

1.2 Ford Delaney Creek

1.6 Young Lakes Trail junction; keep left

4.0 Cross twin bridges over the Tuolumne River

5.3 Junction with May Lake / McGee Lake Trail; turn right

5.6 Glen Aulin High Sierra Camp

8.9 Waterwheel Falls

10.2 Cross Return Creek

14.7 Cross Register Creek, then Rodgers Creek

19.5 Piute Creek junction; go straight into Pate Valley

26.7 First Harden Lake junction

28.2 Harden Lake

29.1 White Wolf

Waterfalls of the
Sierra Crest

The scenery changes dramatically this high up on the crest of the Sierra Nevada. The great open expanses of meadow and rock, the thin air, high winds, and intense sun are intimidating to some visitors, while others are overcome by the (usually ill-advised) urge to burst into song. The forest only occurs in welcoming clumps of whitebark pines, gnarled and full of personality. The very ground underfoot is different up here. Instead of the massive granitic rock of the western slope, sections of the Sierra crest known as a roof pendant are made of ancient multicolored metamorphic rock that breaks into slabs and chunks, changing the way the snowmelt flows over and through the rocks in interesting patterns. The views down to the Owens Valley and the volcanic desert country around Mono Lake are so wildly different from the mountain meadows and conifers to the west, it feels as though you could be gazing at another planet.

There are more cascades than free-falling waterfalls, more complex courses for meltwater to take, more contrasting colors for striking photos. There is lots of wildlife to see here too, like bighorn sheep, marmots, pikas, Belding ground squirrels, outsized alpine hares, and big raucous jays called Clark's nutcrackers.

The Sierra crest marks the northeastern border of Yosemite, and some of the hikes to the waterfalls described here straddle the boundary of the park. All of these waterfalls are found at elevations above 9,000 feet, so they are not accessible in winter except by snowshoes or cross-country skis. But if you can get to some of them in early spring when roads have first opened and the falls are still frozen, some take the form of elaborate, many-tiered wedding cakes.

Tioga Pass, on CA 120, the eastern entrance to Yosemite, is the highest highway pass in California, at 9,943 feet, and is the only auto route into the park from the east. It is subject to avalanches and closes after the first heavy winter snow, usually in November, and does not reopen until May or June. From the west side of the Sierra, the Tioga Road is closed above Crane Flat in winter. The Tioga Road leaves US 395 and begins to climb westward just south of the town of Lee Vining and 30 miles north of Mammoth Lakes. The route is steep and winding and spectacular. During the summer all of the roads to trailheads for these hikes and waterfalls are accessible

Falls in Lundy Canyon originate in high late-melting snowfields.

to ordinary passenger cars with normal clearance, though some are not paved. There is no longer any gasoline in Tuolumne Meadow so make sure you fill up before you head up the mountain.

Note: This country takes getting used to. Symptoms of altitude sickness like headache and nausea are common while your body adjusts to the thin air up here. Give yourself a day or two to acclimatize before vigorous activity if you are coming from near sea level.

47 Mill Creek Falls

Lundy Canyon is just outside the Yosemite border. It is part of the Hoover Wilderness but is well known to those who love Yosemite and is included here because of its many and beautiful waterfalls, as well as one of the finest wildflower displays and the most brilliant fall colors anywhere. There is a fascinating and active beaver colony that was at least partly destroyed by the heavy snow of the winter of 2016–17. This was a productive mining area in the 1880s. You can hike up the canyon as far as you like; there is something interesting at every step, but most exciting of all are its waterfalls. The best and most accessible are on Mill Creek, rushing down alongside the trail, where you can choose from among several picnic and photography spots.

Height of falls: Indeterminate
Start: Lundy Canyon Trailhead in the Lundy Campground
Distance: 5.0 miles out and back
Hiking time: 2 hours to all day
Elevation change: About 600 feet
Difficulty: Easy to moderate, depending on how far you go
Seasons: Summer through fall, though falls are best and most numerous June–July
Nearest facilities: Toilets, food, water at Lundy Lake Resort. Pit toilet at the trailhead.
Permits: None

Maps: USGS Dunderberg Peak quad
Special considerations: In the past it was possible to continue to the top of the bowl containing Mill Creek, climbing to Helen Lake, and continuing over Lundy Pass to wind up at Saddlebag Lakes in 20 Lakes Basin and from there into Yosemite (where you would need a shuttle back to the Lundy trailhead). The old trail still shows on the topo map, and people do occasionally try it, but it has not been maintained in years and the footing is unstable and very dangerous now.

Finding the trailhead: From US 395 take the Lundy Lake turnoff 7 miles north of Lee Vining. Drive west 5 miles to the far end of Lundy Lake. Where the road forks just below the lake, keep right. Pass the tiny general store and continue for about a mile on a narrow, bumpy road through a primitive campground to where the road makes a one-way loop, at the end of which are a few parking spaces. Trailhead GPS: N38 01.20' / W119 15.42'

The Hike

Begin following a level path through a quaking aspen forest and continue along the northeast slope of Lundy Canyon above Mill Creek on colorful red, black, and white rock. A very active population of beavers had dammed the lower part of the creek in several places to create some very large ponds (damaged during the snowy winter of 2016–17), but eventually the slope becomes too steep and the stream too rapid for the dams as it drops over the first of several sets of small waterfalls. At times the trail skirts the bank, at others it climbs above the creek over colorful red, black, and white metamorphic rock and winds around shaggy, sculptural junipers.

Mill Creek has lots of little ledges where you can eat lunch.

The first real waterfall you'll see is really a pair of noisy side-by-side cascades racing one another down the canyon. In about a mile beyond these, cross a side creek on logs amid a riotously blooming flower garden, then follow a level stretch of trail through more aspen forest. After crossing another branch of the creek, sometimes dry, sometimes deep enough to require a log crossing, pass the remains of an old miner's cabin at mile 1.5, beyond which the trail begins to climb the slope above Mill Creek.

Once you're clear of the dense aspen forest, watch for the slender silver threads of water pouring hundreds of feet down the sides of the barren, rocky red bowl from sometimes hidden snowfields. Ignore any apparent trails that cut away from the main route as you continue alongside the creek for less than a mile where a series of beautiful stairstep cascades begins. You can find a number of idyllic spots, each just a few steps off the trail, where quiet pools lined with flowers alternate with perfectly proportioned little waterfalls, each more beautiful than the last. Be sure to watch for dippers, little brown birds that perform a series of vigorous streamside squats, then walk right into *and under* the water to feed on creatures that live on the creek bottom.

After every stop you will probably be tempted to climb just a little higher to take one more photo, to see what just one more cascade is like, until the vegetation

Mill Creek Falls

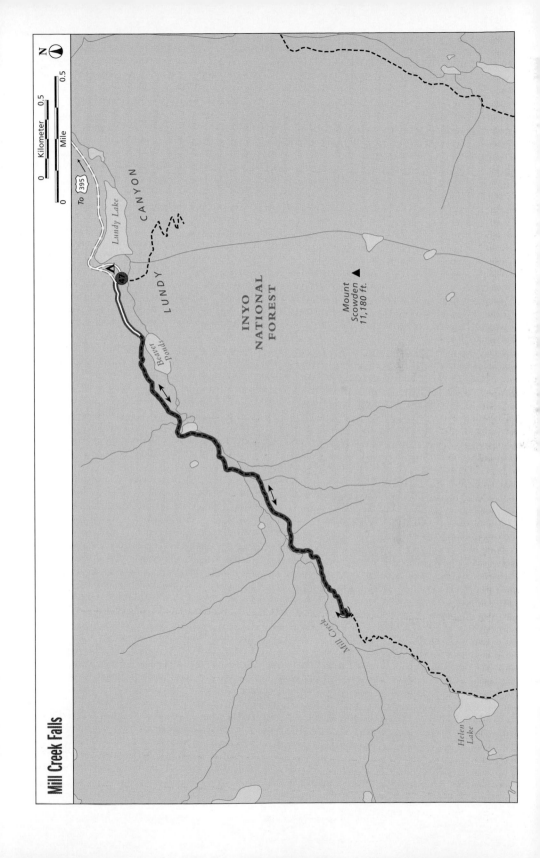

The water from these falls is captured downstream by a beaver colony.

becomes too dense, the grade too steep, or the hour too late and you must head back to the trailhead.

Miles and Directions

0.0 Lundy Canyon Trailhead

0.7 First waterfalls

1.5 Miner's cabin

2.5 Mill Creek cascades

5.0 Arrive back at the trailhead

◄ *In one glance you can see several different falls in Lundy Canyon.*

48 Parker Pass Falls

Dozens of unnamed falls and cascades tinkle and tumble and roar down from melting snowfields tucked into shady niches in the alpine country of Yosemite's northeast borderlands. Some of these snowfields will vanish by midsummer, but many remain late into the season. They feed small turquoise-colored pools that glisten among multicolored metamorphic rocks decorated with miniature wildflower gardens. Beyond these are spine-tingling views all the way down to Mono Lake in the Owens Valley. It's a wild world up here, inhospitable in appearance, but unsurpassed in scenic beauty. If you are lucky, you might get to watch a herd of bighorn sheep negotiating the impossible cliffs. Campsites are limited here because the area is rocky and often wet, but there are a few flat, protected spots, and the views are worth any discomfort. Strong hikers can do this as a day hike but are guaranteed to wish they had more time to spend here.

Height of falls: Variable
Start: Mono Pass Trailhead
Distance: 13.0 miles out and back
Hiking time: 7–8 hours or overnight
Elevation change: At least 2,000 feet each way
Difficulty: Moderate as a backpack, strenuous as a day hike
Seasons: Summer, whenever the Tioga Road is open
Nearest facilities: Toilets but no water at the trailhead; food, water, phones at Tuolumne Meadows; gas at Lee Vining

Permits: None for a day hike; available for overnights in advance or at the Tuolumne Meadows Wilderness Center
Maps: USGS Koip Peak and Tioga Pass quads
Special considerations: The entire watershed of the Dana Fork of the Tuolumne River is closed to camping since it is the source of drinking water for Tuolumne Meadows. So you must go beyond Parker Pass to pitch your tent. You are above timberline here with rocky or soggy ground underfoot and not much shelter. Give yourself enough time to seek out a more-or-less dry and comfortable spot if you plan to spend the night. Fires are prohibited.

Finding the trailhead: From the Tioga Road (CA 120), drive about 12 miles east of Tuolumne Meadows or a little more than a mile west of the Tioga Pass Entrance Station to the marked Mono Pass Trailhead. There are bear boxes and parking spaces that fill up early. Trailhead GPS: N37 53.27' / W119 15.45'

The Hike

The trail winds its way generally southwestward through lodgepole pine forest alternating with little fingers of Dana Meadow, where you might have to wade or rock-hop an early season creek. Just beyond, the trail swings left (east), climbing through more forest and meadow. The bulky granite mass to the right is Mammoth Peak,

Many of the cascades on Parker Pass are trimmed in wildflowers.

the northern culmination of the Kuna Crest. (Don't confuse this with Mammoth Mountain, the ski resort south of Yosemite.)

At mile 1.3 the remains of an old pioneer cabin slouch beside the trail, and at about the same time, you pick up the gurgling of Parker Pass Creek on the right. Following the creek upstream, you cross a tributary stream feeding the main creek amid a dense exhalation of swamp onions, and just beyond, at mile 2.3, you meet a junction with the Spillway Lake Trail that angles off to the south, taking Parker Pass Creek with it. Your trail continues southeast and the grade steepens. As you climb, you get glimpses across the valley of the light-gray Kuna Crest to the right with a colorful strip of red metamorphic rock at its base, a foretaste of things to come.

At 3.0 miles pass a rockslide that used to be alive with scurrying, squeaking pikas, little alpine rabbit relatives that seem to be disappearing from many of their usual High Sierra haunts, probably due to rising temperatures. Pass a second tumbledown cabin. Just beyond it the forest opens to reveal red Mount Lewis at the head of the meadow. At mile 3.4 follow the signed Parker Pass Trail as it cuts off to the right (south) across sometimes marshy ground between shallow lakes.

Climb up a rocky ridge dotted with whitebark pines that gradually disappear as you reach treeline and watch out for Spillway Lake in a shallow basin on your right (west). Continue up a gradual slope until you top out at windswept Parker Pass at 11,100 feet, where you leave Yosemite Park. This pass is marked by a small forest of trail signs. If you have the time and energy, make a short detour from the pass and

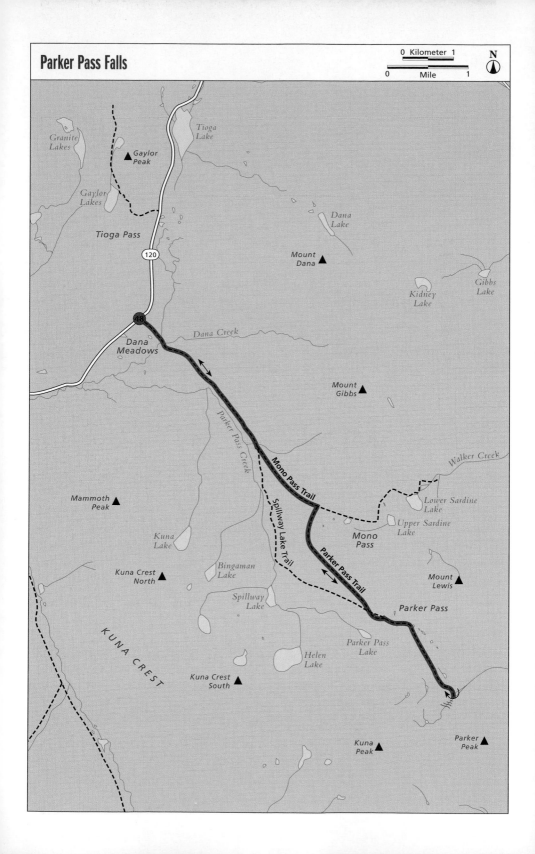

Parker Pass Falls

Granite Lakes
Gaylor Peak
Tioga Lake
Gaylor Lakes
Tioga Pass
Dana Lake
Mount Dana
120
Kidney Lake
Gibbs Lake
48
Dana Creek
Dana Meadows
Mount Gibbs
Parker Pass Creek
Walker Creek
Mono Pass Trail
Mammoth Peak
Spillway Lake Trail
Lower Sardine Lake
Upper Sardine Lake
Mono Pass
Kuna Lake
Parker Pass Trail
Kuna Crest North
Bingaman Lake
Mount Lewis
Spillway Lake
Parker Pass
KUNA CREST
Parker Pass Lake
Helen Lake
Kuna Crest South
Kuna Peak
Parker Peak

0 Kilometer 1
0 Mile 1
N

All the Parker Pass cascades come from melting snow.

descend the slope on your right to discover hidden Parker Pass Lake tucked into a declivity below the trail.

About a half mile beyond the pass, you descend down a series of terraces where you can wander, or sometimes scramble, along a chain of cascades connecting a string of little silver or blue ponds trimmed with miniature gardens of yellow monkey flowers, white mountain heather, pink elephant heads, and sky-blue lupines.

The terraces continue on down to a low point from which the trail climbs a daunting series of switchbacks up to Koip Pass.

The trail passes from one terrace to another, each one with its own flavor. About three terraces down a gully hold snow well into summer, and the meltwater from this one spreads out in a very broad but shallow fan, where you'll probably get wet feet.

These snowfields are at such high elevation that they last far into summer.

The snowfield above is cut into intricate designs around its borders and is sometimes broken into what look like big continental plates in a geology textbook. Between these plates roar great gushes of water.

It's a noisy place with multiple small rivers crashing over the stones. It's one of the most dramatic environments you'll ever experience. The blinding white snow and shining watercourses against the background of dark metamorphic rocks provide a real challenge for photographers.

Eventually, reluctantly, you will have to return the way you came.

Miles and Directions

0.0 Mono Pass Trailhead
2.3 Spillway Lake Trail junction; keep left
3.4 Parker Pass Trail junction; turn right
5.3 Parker Pass
6.5 Parker Pass waterfall basin
13.0 Arrive back at Mono Pass Trailhead

Option: You can take a side trip to Mono Pass, Sardine Lakes, Bloody Canyon, and Mono Lake viewpoints. At the Parker Pass turnoff, continue straight ahead on the Mono Pass Trail for another 0.4 mile (0.3 according to the sign), passing a series of lakes set in green meadows early in the season, golden grasses later on, to signed Mono Pass. Descend into the Ansel Adams Wilderness, passing Sardine Lake as you enter steep and rocky Bloody Canyon. From several points beside the trail, you can scramble up just a few steps to see unearthly Mono Lake, part of the Owens Valley, and the White Mountains beyond.

49 Ellery Lake Falls

Ellery Lake Falls are sometimes called Lee Vining Falls, since they flow down the narrow gorge of Lee Vining Canyon to the Poole Power Plant below when Southern California Edison opens the gates below Ellery Lake. The official height is 70 feet, but the falls' total descent to the floor of Lee Vining Canyon is much greater.

The falls are seldom completely dry but often only drizzle down in two skinny streams. It's the long, long drop against the backdrop of beautiful red cliffs behind them that attracts attention. When the falls are flowing, though, they hurtle down the narrow gorge of Lee Vining Canyon in a fury, and the scenic overlooks are always occupied during those times. You can see it all from a distance, but if you enjoy the sensation of butterflies in your stomach, park your car and take this hike to the far side of the gorge when the water is roaring.

The Tioga Pass Road is closed in winter, but if you arrive just after the pass opens in spring, the falls may form several magical ice castles as sheets from the spray frost the walls of the gorge. You can get great views of these if you snowshoe or ski up the Tioga Road.

Height of falls: Their official measurement is 70 feet, but there are cascades more than 1,500 feet down.
Start: Parking area on the north side of the Ellery Lake Dam
Distance: About 2.4 miles out and back
Hiking time: 1 hour

Elevation change: 100 feet
Difficulty: Easy
Seasons: Spring and summer, whenever the Tioga Road is open
Nearest facilities: Lee Vining
Permits: None
Maps: USGS Mount Dana quad

Finding the trailhead: From the west at the Tioga Pass entrance to Yosemite, follow the Tioga Road (CA 120) down (east) about 8 to 10 miles to the dam at the lower end of signed Ellery Lake. From US 395 head west up CA 120 to the lower end of Ellery Lake and stop at any of the turnouts where everybody else has stopped to marvel at the waterfall. If you plan to hike, park at the turnout nearest the dam. Trailhead GPS: N37 56.12' / W119 13.52'

The Hike

You can enjoy the falls from several turnouts on the upper part of CA 120. If water is being released from Ellery Lake and is thundering down the canyon to the Poole Power Plant, you're in luck and will have plenty of company at each turnout. A little farther up the road, the long, slender streamer of water flowing into the lake from above is too far away for pictures, even with a telephoto lens, but it is a very long, skinny, and very impressive waterfall that lasts until the snowfield near the ridgeline has melted.

Ellery Lake Falls are interesting even when water is not being released.

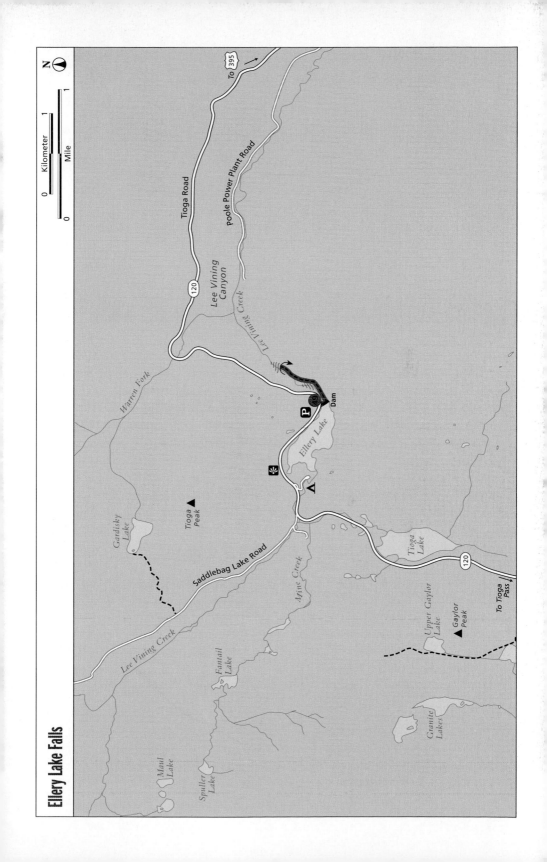

Ellery Lake Falls

The icy cliffs above Ellery Lake are popular challenges for climbers.

To really see the falls below the lake as almost nobody else does, park in the turnout on CA 120 nearest the dam. Walk through an open gate and cross to the opposite side, where a faint anglers trail turns right along the lakeshore. A sign warns everyone that this is Southern California Edison territory and that you will be hiking at your own risk. Your route follows a rough road heading away from the lake to the left. You can't see this road from the highway and it isn't shown on the map, so you'll probably have it to yourself. The road does not follow right along the rim but leaves a low barrier of boulders between you and the abyss. There are gaps where you can peer through the low places at the waterfall, but be cautious when scrambling over slippery, glacially polished granite. There is always a stream of water in the gorge, but if you're lucky and water is being released from Ellery Lake, the torrent is furious and deafening.

In the late fall or early spring when the road might be open or, better, in midwinter if you're willing to ski or snowshoe up Tioga Road, you can watch ice climbers inching their way up the frozen waterfalls across the gorge. In summer look for occasional pairs of bolts drilled into the rocks where climbers anchor their ropes.

You can follow this road for a mile or two, then turn around when your butterflies, or your feet, get tired.

Miles and Directions

0.0 Trailhead at Ellery Lake Dam

0.2 After crossing the dam, turn left on gravel road

1.2 Continue along the gravel road above the gorge until the fall is no longer visible

2.4 Arrive back at the trailhead

50 West Lake Falls

There are two sets of waterfalls at West Lake, one at its inlet, the other at the outlet. In fact, there are two lakes as well. The trail takes you directly to the first, smaller pool and the top of the waterfall at its outlet. The trail gives out before the second, much larger West Lake, but you can get a good view of the inlet waterfall at the far end. Both of these lakes, along with Green Lake just below, are full of trout and very popular with anglers.

Height of fall: 900 feet
Start: Green Creek Trailhead
Distance: 7.0 miles out and back
Hiking time: 5–6 hours or overnight
Elevation change: 1,900 feet
Difficulty: Moderately strenuous as a day hike, strenuous as a backpack

Season: July–Sept
Nearest facilities: Bridgeport or Lee Vining; toilets but no potable water at the trailhead
Permits: None needed for a day hike, available in advance or first-come, first-served from the Hoover Wilderness Office at Bridgeport
Maps: USGS Dunderberg Peak quad

Finding the trailhead: Drive about 9 miles up from CA 120 on Green Creek Road. At an unmarked corner, make a very sharp turn to the right. There are few signs here, so you'll have to watch for a sharper-than-a-hairpin turn. If you are not sure about the turn, the way straight ahead goes gently downhill, while your route goes up. You will have a couple of miles of bumpy washboard surface. Pass an extensive area of beaver activity with complicated channels and dams, and after this ends watch for the trailhead on your right. It usually has plenty of cars in it, along with a toilet. If you reach the campground, you have gone too far.

The Hike

The trail goes around the back and above the campground (the road the campground is on is actually shorter and hugs the creek, but there is nowhere to park there unless you have reserved a campsite). In a mile reach a signed junction where the road to the campground meets the road to the trailhead to find your way back. Climb with the stream (Green Creek) tumbling noisily alongside, often hidden behind aspens. The terrain alternates between aspen and pine forest and open rock. Sometimes the grade is fairly steep, but it is usually moderate. The trail rambles alongside Green Creek through dense quaking-aspen groves and lots of water-loving wildflowers at first, then climbs steeply beside a series of noisy cascades. A sign marks the entrance to the Hoover Wilderness as you continue to ascend steadily to a junction with the West Lake and Green Lake Trails at 2.0 miles. In another 0.3 mile or so, a second junction points downhill toward Green Lake, but you keep heading to the right. Green Lake has plenty of good campsites if you want to spend the night, but the Forest Service stocks these lakes with trout and you'll have lots of neighbors, mostly anglers.

West Lake Falls stand out sharply against red rock.

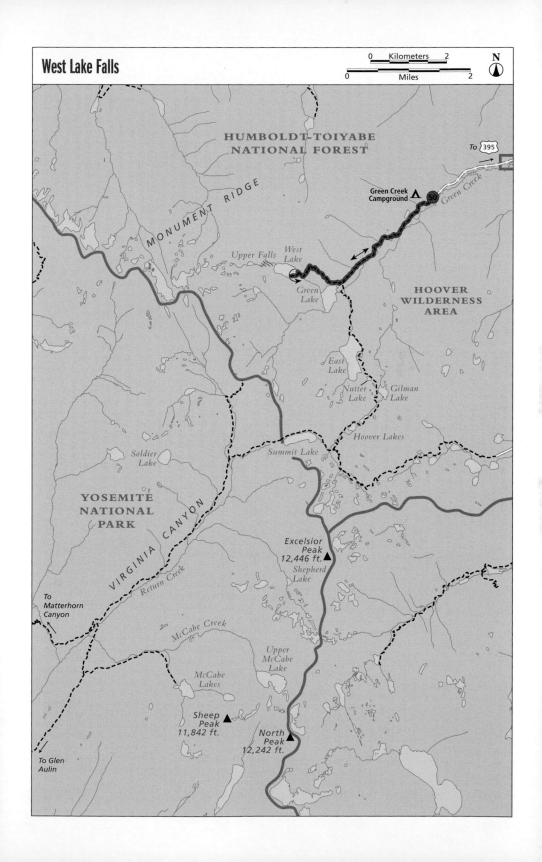

West Lake Falls

0 Kilometers 2
0 Miles 2

N

HUMBOLDT-TOIYABE
NATIONAL FOREST

To 395

Green Creek
Campground

50

Green Creek

MONUMENT RIDGE

Upper Falls

West
Lake

Green
Lake

HOOVER
WILDERNESS
AREA

East
Lake

Nutter
Lake

Gilman
Lake

Hoover Lakes

Soldier
Lake

Summit Lake

YOSEMITE
NATIONAL
PARK

VIRGINIA CANYON

Excelsior
Peak
12,446 ft.

Shepherd
Lake

Return Creek

To
Matterhorn
Canyon

McCabe Creek

Upper
McCabe
Lake

McCabe
Lakes

Sheep
Peak
11,842 ft.

North
Peak
12,242 ft.

To Glen
Aulin

This shoulder of land blocks West Lake from Son of West Lake.

Admire the rugged skyline created by Monument Ridge and Gabbro Peak as you climb up a rocky ridge, but remember to glance back into the bowl on your left to see the interesting shoreline and sometimes beautiful reflection of Green Lake.

The trail climbs steadily partly through a mixed forest, with a remarkable variety of conifers. There are Jeffrey pines, lodgepole pines, mountain hemlocks, an occasional western white pine, an occasional juniper, and, as you gain altitude, whitebark pines frequented by squawking Clark's nutcrackers. The forest sections alternate with open stands of tobacco brush and sagebrush. As you head northwest, long, long, silvery, sometimes divided strands of West Lake Falls come into view, dramatically contrasting with the rich red of the metamorphic rocks. You can't get very close to the falls, but the view is impressive. Then the trail makes a turn to the southwest and switchbacks over rough talus as you skirt the ridge separating you from West Lake beyond. In the final half mile, the switchbacks become shorter and steeper, until at mile 3.2 you turn a corner and find yourself at the outlet to a little dolphin-shaped lake that ought to be West Lake but isn't. The real West Lake is much bigger and is hidden behind a low ridge. Both of these bodies of water are teeming with trout. From Son of West Lake, you can wander a few yards downstream to have a look at the lake's outlet, which is the top of the waterfall you have been admiring, but you can't see all the way down.

◀   *This is as much as you can see from the top of the falls.*

These lakes are teeming with trout.

To see the real West Lake, go just past a rock dam with an old wooden sluice that used to control the flow of the lake's runoff. The willows on the far side are too dense to penetrate, but you can go downhill a few yards to a little meadow and rock-hop or wade the stream there.

Once across, you can fairly easily make your way across the ridge concealing West Lake at mile 3.5. There is no trail from here, but you can make your way around the western shore and find a high spot where you can get a good view of West Lake's inlet, its second waterfall.

Miles and Directions

0.0 Green Creek Trailhead

1.0 Enter Hoover Wilderness

2.0 Junction with Green Lake and West Lake; keep right

2.3 Second junction with Green Lake; keep right again

3.2 Reach Son of West Lake and cross the inlet

3.5 View of West Lake and its inlet waterfall

7.0 Arrive back at the trailhead

51 Cooney Lake Falls

Cooney Lake Falls isn't named on the map, and it isn't very big, but it is one of the most perfect, picturesque descents through one of the prettiest flower gardens anywhere. You can find it in the Virginia Lakes basin on a high-elevation climb through a cluster of timberline tarns. The basin and this cascade are actually just outside the Yosemite border, but they are part of a convenient and scenic route to many more hikes into the north boundary country of the park. Early in the summer dozens of high snowfields send silver streamers down the red cliffs of the eastern escarpment of the Sierra. Most don't have names and don't flow all year, but if you love waterfalls, you shouldn't miss these.

Height of falls: 80 feet
Start: Virginia Lakes Trailhead
Distance: 3.6 miles out and back
Hiking time: 2-3 hours
Elevation change: 600 feet
Difficulty: Moderate due to elevation at trailhead

Season: Summer into early fall
Nearest facilities: Campground, pack station, store, cafe, lodge, and phone at Virginia Lakes
Permits: None
Maps: USGS Dunderberg Peak quad

Finding the trailhead: From US 395 at Conway Summit north of Mono Lake, take Virginia Lakes Road west for 6 miles. Beyond the pack station the road forks; to the left is a small lodge, store, and cafe; to the right is the USDA Trumbull Lake Campground, and beyond that, the marked trailhead and hikers' parking lot. Trailhead GPS: N38.02.58' / W119 15.49'

The Hike

The trail begins at the biggest of the Virginia Lakes, usually dotted with anglers and paddlers. Your trail climbs gradually through rabbitbrush and sagebrush and comes to a junction at a wilderness sign. Keep left. The trail splits again, but the two forks eventually rejoin. The left follows the lakeside, the other offers a higher view. There is nothing subtle about this scenery. While most of the basin containing the brilliant sapphire of the lake is gray granite, Dunderberg Peak to your right (north) is red, and Black Mountain to the left (south) is black. White snow patches and green clumps of forest make this basin a favorite with color photographers. *Note:* Camping is prohibited at Virginia, Blue, and Red Lakes.

The trail enters the Hoover Wilderness and climbs around the north shore of Blue Lake into a sparse forest of whitebark pines, and you soon pass a tumbledown miner's log cabin on the left. Hop an outlet stream from Moat Lake out of sight above, then, as you approach Cooney Lake, watch for an unmarked path on your left heading downhill toward the lakeside, and follow the sound of rushing water to the

Cooney Lake Falls

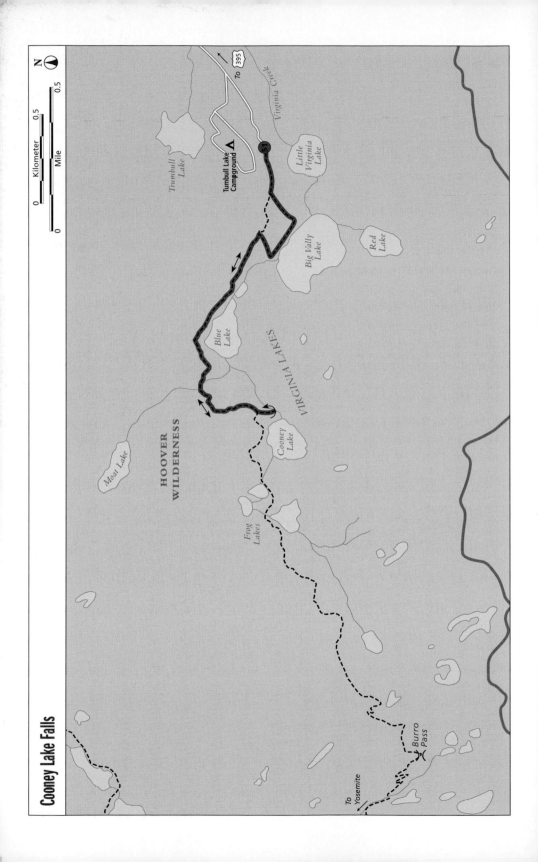

N

0   0.5   Kilometer
0   0.5   Mile

To 395

Virginia Creek

Trumbull Lake

Tumbull Lake Campground

Little Virginia Lake

Big Valley Lake

Red Lake

Blue Lake

VIRGINIA LAKES

Moat Lake

HOOVER WILDERNESS

Cooney Lake

Frog Lakes

Burro Pass

To Yosemite

▶ The rocky slope beside Blue Lake is home to a colony of pikas, busy little earth-colored creatures related to rabbits, which scamper over the rocks of the high country all summer, cutting plant material to store in their burrows under the rubble for winter use. The bundles of grass they carry as they scurry over the talus makes them appear to have huge green mustaches. You can hear their sharp chirps of alarm as you approach, but they become invisible when immobile. If you stand quietly for a few minutes until they decide you are not dangerous, they will resume their activities.

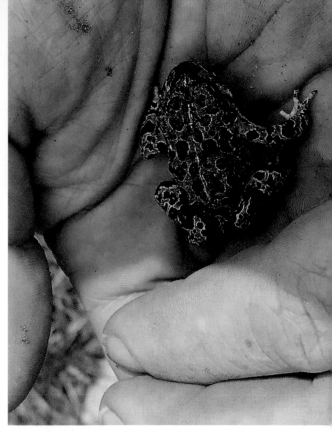

This rare and threatened Yosemite Toad, unlike other toads, is active during the day.

base of "Cooney Lake Falls." These are perfectly proportioned little cascades with a (sometimes damp) grassy viewing/photographing area at the base.

You will probably never want to leave this spot, but should you crave more exercise, head back to the main trail and continue climbing past the shallow Frog Lakes, finally puffing up the final open switchbacks to the pass at 3.3 miles. (This pass is unnamed on the USGS topographic maps but is known as "Burro Pass" to locals. There is another "real" officially named Burro Pass to the west near Matterhorn Peak, so don't get them mixed up.) Retrace your steps back to the trailhead at Virginia Lake.

Miles and Directions

0.0 Virginia Lakes Trailhead
1.0 Wilderness sign; keep left
1.7 Unmarked turnoff on left above Cooney Lake
1.8 Cooney Lake Falls
3.6 Arrive back at the trailhead

Cooney Lake Falls feeds a colorful early season garden in mostly barren upper Virginia Canyon.

Bibliography

Dictionary of Geological Terms. The American Geological Institute. Garden City, NY: Anchor Press, 1976.

Giacomazzi, Sharon. *Trails & Tales of Yosemite & the Central Sierra*. Mendocino, CA: Bored Feet, 2001.

Glazner, Allen F., and Greg M. Stock. *Geology Underfoot in Yosemite National Park*. Missoula, MT: Mountain Press Pub. Co., 2010.

Historical records by Clark, S. A. Barrett.

Huber, N. King. *The Geologic Story of Yosemite National Park*, USGS Bulletin 1595, 1987.

Kroeber, A. L. *Handbook of the Indians of California*. Reprint edition. Mineola, NY: Dover Publications, 2012. Originally published by the Government Printing Office, Washington, DC: Bulletin of American Ethnology of the Smithsonian Institution, 1925.

Peppin, William A. *The Waterfalls of Yosemite During Big Water*. Self-published, 2011.

Storer, Tracy L., Robert L Usinger, and David Lucas. *Sierra Nevada Natural History*. Berkeley and Los Angeles: University of California Press, 2004.

Swedo, Suzanne. *Hiking Yosemite National Park*. Guilford, CT: Falcon Guides, 2016.

Worldwaterfalldatabase.com

YourOwnHike.com

About the Author

Suzanne Swedo has taught natural science seminars for the Yosemite Conservancy in Yosemite National Park for more than thirty years. During the same period she has conducted wilderness survival, outdoor skills, and natural history outings as founder and director of W.I.L.D., an international and domestic adventure travel company. She has also led nature and wilderness trips for various educational organizations including the University of California Extension, the National Outings Program of the Sierra Club, Wilderness Institute, Pacific Wilderness Institute, and Outdoor Adventures.

Suzanne has demonstrated wilderness skills in a ten-week television series called *Alive and Well* and served as a survival consultant for Warner Bros. Television. Her writings on travel and the outdoors have appeared in such publications as the *Los Angeles Examiner* and *California Magazine*. Other books for FalconGuides are *Hiking Yosemite National Park*, *Wilderness Survival*, *Hiking the Hawaiian Islands*, and *Best Easy Day Hikes Yosemite National Park*.

She has backpacked the mountains of every continent.

RICK SMITH PHOTO